Landscaping in Florida
A Photo Idea Book

NATURE'S INVITATION—Flat chunks of granite set in a Boca Ciega Bay rock garden invite the casual visitor to enter this seaside garden and listen to the musical duet of whistling myrtles against the whisper of surf on sand.

Residence of Mr. and Mrs. Harold C. Anderson, St. Petersburg

Landscaping in Florida
A Photo Idea Book

by Mac Perry

Pineapple Press
Sarasota, Florida

Published by Pineapple Press, Inc., P.O. 3899, Sarasota, Florida 34230.

Library of Congress Cataloging-in-Publication Data

Perry, Mac.
   Landscaping in Florida.

   Includes Index.
   1. Landscape gardening—Florida. 2. Landscape architecture—Florida.
3. Landscape gardening—Florida—Pictorial works. 4. Landscape architecture–
Florida–Pictorial works. I. Title
SB472.32.U6P47   1989   712'.09759   88-28875
ISBN 1-56164-057-3

Printed in Hong Kong
Design by Frank Cochrane Associates, Sarasota, Florida
Illustrations by Mac Perry, Bob Weaver, and Frank Cochrane

With special thanks and dedication to horticulturist
Gil Whitton, who gave me so much in those early years

Contents

FOREST OR LANDSCAPED LAWN?—The boughs of aged live oaks (*Quercus virginiana*) point in every direction as the lone traveler strides through this mini tropical forest that appears to have landscaped itself. Many designers feel the closer you can duplicate nature the better you will enjoy your landscape. Surely Mr. and Mrs. Harold C. Anderson of St. Petersburg would agree. This is their side yard.

Introduction

SPECIAL PROBLEMS AND ADVANTAGES IN THE FLORIDA LANDSCAPE—Florida *is* different. As any Florida gardener can tell you, this state boasts the greatest collection of enemies to the landscape in the entire United States. Our plants have more diseases than plants in California and Texas because of our high humidity, which tends to spread diseases more rapidly. And we have more insects because we do not have the long, hard freeze of our northern neighbors. Such freezes often kill off huge populations of insects, forcing them to repopulate from a minimum of survivors in the spring. And we have the ever-persistent nematode, a microscopic worm that feeds in and on the roots of almost all plants. About a dozen harmful species of nematodes thrive in warm Florida soils and are very difficult to control.

The Florida environment has even more plant enemies: sandy soils that force us to rely on costly irrigation systems (two deep waterings a week produce deep-rooted, healthy plants while daily watering promotes shallow roots, weed growth, and the spread of diseases), hammock peat in the southern sections that retains too much water for healthy plant growth, low nutrient levels due to our lack of valleys and the gentle slope of our terrain from the central range to the Gulf and Atlantic, imbalanced nutrient and pH conditions (as in the phosphate regions near Tampa Bay), and the high shell content of our shoreline cities.

Conditions are compounded when we experience long hot summers that kill off northern shrubs we try to import, unexpected freezes that destroy south Florida plants growing in central Florida, and extended drought periods followed by weeks of torrential inundations. All are compounded by the salty soil and salt drift experienced in our coastal areas.

On the other hand, nowhere in America can we find such diversity of landscape plant material to work with. From the tropics and from Europe we have gathered a splendid collection of unusual and superb plants of exquisite beauty. Each day people move into Florida and make their homes here. And with them come ideas and influences that when superimposed upon our surroundings—already heavily influenced by the early Spanish, English, and French settlers, the native Indians, as well as our nearby Caribbean neighbors—produce an environment of great diversity unrivaled anywhere in America. This diversity is seen in our architecture, along our streets, and especially in our landscapes where personalized touches are most evident. Each little garden and entryway reveals its own influence.

WHAT THIS BOOK OFFERS—In this volume I present a survey of practical and pleasing landscape ideas found throughout the state. Emphasis is placed on residences showing what homeowners and professional landscapers have done and can do with these ideas. From north Florida with its cold-tolerant plants, spring burst of bloom, and spacious wooded home lots, through central Florida with its unique combination of both temperate and tropic plants, to the jungles of south Florida with its blaze of year-round color, you will discover a wealth of ideas you can put to use in your own homescape.

Besides residential home ideas you will find special sections on landscaping offices, commercial buildings, city streets, parks, and mobile homes. There are numerous construction ideas for using wood and concrete. I have offered many ways to make the landscape more functional since that must be a common goal along with making it more beautiful. Chapter Seven offers scores of plant descriptions to help you make plant choices. Complete botanical names as well as common names, heights, zones, and notes are found in this reference chapter. Chapter Three offers many ideas on working in color.

THE GROUND RULES—As in all arts, there are rules in landscaping that help produce a finer art. The rules of landscaping are better called guidelines since that is what they are. The ultimate goal is the development of outdoor spaces into attractive, functional areas. These guidelines include the principles of design (balance, contrast, texture, etc.), using pressure-treated lumber and galvanized nails for long-lasting outdoor decks, creating transition areas between the home and the lawn, providing good traffic flow throughout the landscape, and a host of other techniques you will find throughout the text.

You will note that some of the plants grow in specific zones of the state—north, central, or south—while others thrive in all zones. These are indicated (in Chapter Seven) with the initials N, C, or S. However, the emphasis in this book is on design—the *placement* of plants and special constructions to achieve function and beauty in outdoor living areas. Good design is good anywhere, but plant substitutions may be necessary for north or south zones. Substitutions are easily made by referring to Chapter Seven.

Now sit back and enjoy an armchair landscape tour across Florida and be sure to keep a pencil handy to jot down ideas you can use to enhance the usefulness and beauty of your own landscape.

Now for a little humor in closing, but pay careful attention to the moral:

A parson walks by a colorful and orderly front lawn and shouts across a bed of flowers, "Henry, what a lovely garden you and the Lord have made."

Henry looks up as he pulls the last weed from a border bed. "Parson, you shoulda seen it when the Lord had it by Himself."

Mac Perry

C H A P T E R *One*

LOVELY TO LOOK AT, EASY TO MOW—An open span of lawn provides lots of space for yard games at this lovely woodside residence. Volleyball, croquet, badminton, anyone? Or just relax in the hammock stretched in a shady distant corner. The effect? A pleasing vista and a lawn easy to mow because all plantings are massed separately from the lawn.

Residence: Jim and Marge Mang—Largo

How to make your landscape functional

Landscapes are for people. Before anything else the landscape must fulfill the needs and desires of the people who will use it.

Check your landscape plan to see if mowing maintenance is reduced by planting all trees in beds. Are there easy foot-traffic patterns around both sides of the house—from car to entryway, from house to work area in the yard? Are fence and hedge barriers placed to reduce noise and wind, to hide a poor view? Is the landscape divided into distinct and separate areas like your home—public area for viewing and meeting guests; private area for napping, sunbathing, quiet reading; recreation area for entertainment; work area for vegetable gardening, storage shed, wood pile?

Are plants chosen to provide shade, shield against salt spray, reduce glare, prevent erosion, filter dust from the air, provide privacy? Are walks and drive of adequate size? Are there plenty of construction items to provide shelter and ease of foot-traffic flow? Is a hard surface offered for recreation such as shuffleboard and basketball? Has careful thought been given to choosing plants requiring a minimum of maintenance?

In the words of the Right Honorable William Windham, "Plants are not to be laid out with a view to their appearance in a picture, but to their uses, and the enjoyment of them in real life; and their conformity to those purposes is that which constitutes beauty."

The use of the landscape must be satisfied first. Before designing your landscape, make a list of your needs and those of the land itself. Then choose the plants and constructions that will fulfill those needs. Finally, imagine the placement of plants and constructions in patterns and arrangements that will be aesthetically pleasing. It is this orderly planning of outdoor living spaces that constitutes landscape design and results in the enjoyment of life with and within the landscape.

Here now are some ways that landscape designers in Florida have made landscapes functional.

A beautiful landscape can be functional

A two-car driveway opens onto a spacious walk and "goodnight patio." Foot traffic moves easily around both sides of the house. Viewed from the street the house is well framed with taller plants to the outside. Two trees on the street provide visual depth. A fence along with hedges on the sides and at the rear gives privacy. Function areas are sufficient and well located to match those of the house. There is plenty of hard surface for patio and work areas. The back patio has seclusion and an oblique vista onto an open lawn. The plan provides lots of room for recreation and benches for resting. Foot-traffic flow is exceptional with many provisions for ins and outs. The design is unified, balanced, yet simple.

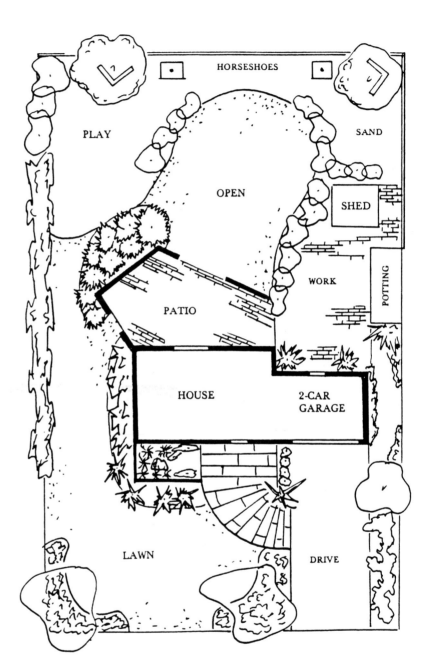

Plants can be functional

Choosing the proper plant for a location is not merely a matter of choosing for beauty. Plants can be used to block wind, shield against salt spray, hide a poor view, direct foot traffic, allow sun to warm the house in winter and block its heat in summer (deciduous trees), keep animals and trespassers off property (mass of low, thorny shrubs), create a micro environment for peaceful isolation and much more.

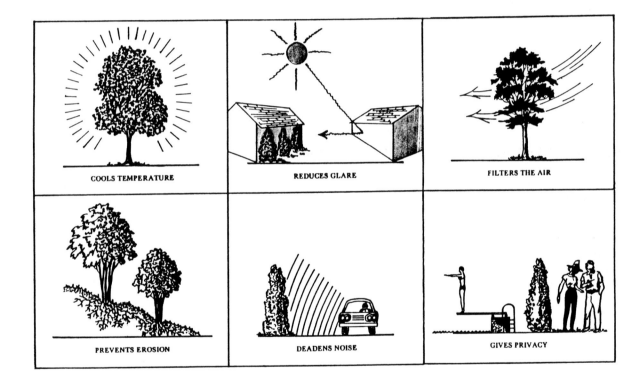

COOLS TEMPERATURE

REDUCES GLARE

FILTERS THE AIR

PREVENTS EROSION

DEADENS NOISE

GIVES PRIVACY

Design a play area

The location of the play area in the landscape should be in clear view of the house so small children can be easily supervised. Locate within this outdoor room all of the recreational facilities desired by the family—horseshoes, swing set, sandbox, and others. The driveway can be extended to provide a hard surface for ball bouncing. The backside of a fence can hold a large, outdoor chalkboard for score-keeping, sketching pictures, or playing tick-tack-toe. Plants in this area should be just a few, hardy species. Dainty little posies are likely to get stomped.

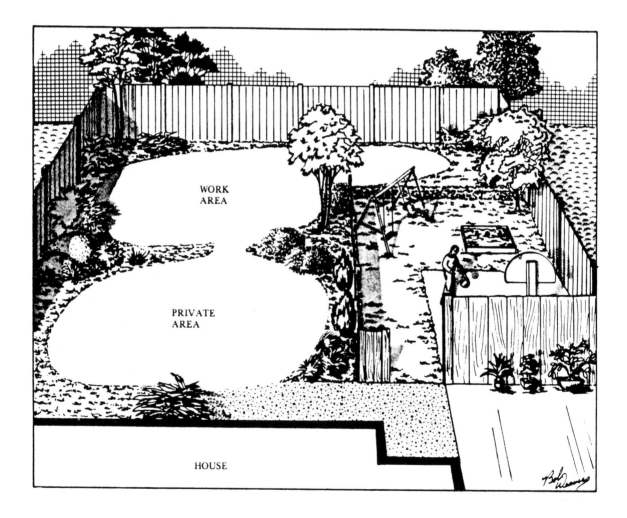

Design a work area

The lawn work area should be near the home's work area (garage, laundry room, kitchen). Give it partial seclusion with fences, hedges or low-growing shrubs. Provide ample room for garbage cans, a vegetable garden, a clothesline, and a storage shed.

PRIVATE AREA

PLAY AREA

Design
a privacy
area

This area should be adjacent to the bedroom side of the home. Because seclusion is the most important factor, taller fences dressed in landscape shrubbery are best.

Provide a firm surface and a soft lawn for sunbathing. Also, a trickling waterfall (for a soothing sound) makes a good addition in this little retreat.

Prepare your own landscape plan

After studying the illustrations, photos, and plant lists in this book you will be ready to prepare your own landscape design plan. The following will show you how to tape an 18″ x 24″ sheet of paper to a drawing board or a smooth-edged table. You will need a "T" square, a 30-60-90 triangle, a 45-45-90 triangle and a ruler. Also, notice the symbols and a typical alphabet that will make your plan more attractive.

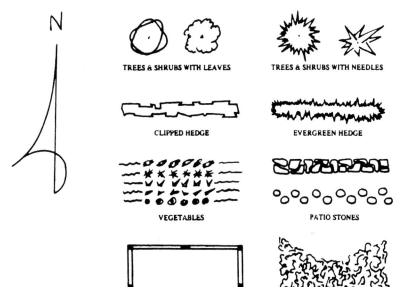

TREES & SHRUBS WITH LEAVES   TREES & SHRUBS WITH NEEDLES

CLIPPED HEDGE   EVERGREEN HEDGE

VEGETABLES   PATIO STONES

FENCE   GROUND COVER

SYMBOLS YOU WILL NEED

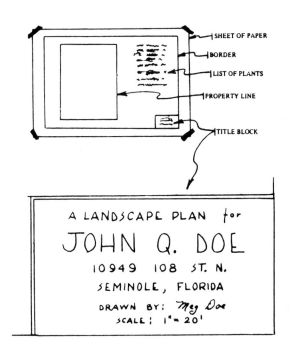

SHEET OF PAPER
BORDER
LIST OF PLANTS
PROPERTY LINE
TITLE BLOCK

A LANDSCAPE PLAN for
JOHN Q. DOE
10949 108 ST. N.
SEMINOLE, FLORIDA
DRAWN BY: Meg Doe
SCALE: 1″ = 20′

DESIGN PLAN SETUP

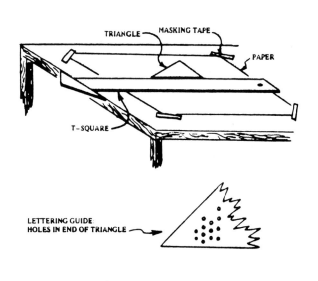

TRIANGLE   MASKING TAPE
PAPER
T-SQUARE
LETTERING GUIDE
HOLES IN END OF TRIANGLE

DESIGN TABLE LAYOUT

Create your own functional and beautiful Florida home landscape in five easy steps

STEP 1—THE EXISTING PLAN

Measure and record on a large sheet of paper the outside dimensions of lot and home. Draw a diagram to scale. Place an arrow pointing north. Show streets, existing walks and drives, and the home's interior floor plan. Then sketch in all existing plants, grass, gravel, poles, fences, clothesline, and other features. Note any special conditions or problems such as faulty gutter downspouts, electric wires that might interfere with growing trees, narrow walkways, plants to be removed or relocated. Drawing this diagram will cause you to closely study the problems and advantages with which you have to work.

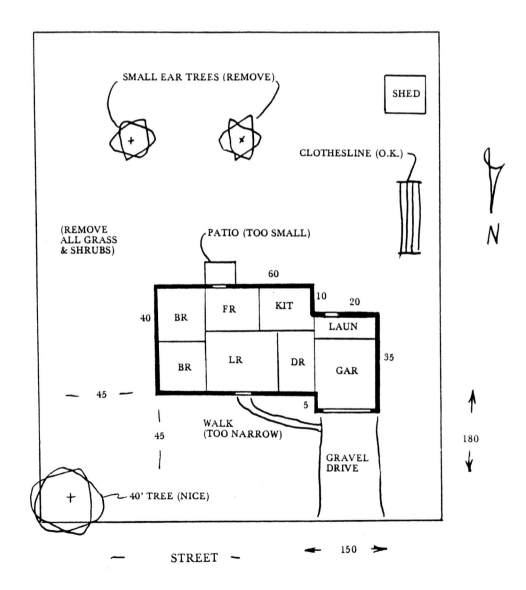

STEP 2—SITE SURVEY PLAN

On another sheet of paper carefully record the site's survey conditions. This is accomplished by walking over the site noticing all desired and undesired views, the direction of prevailing winds, and the movement of the sun in summer and winter (give special attention to the location of the sun in the afternoon when you're likely to use the lawn), foot traffic patterns to, from and around the house. Also locate where barriers are needed to hide a view or to block prevailing wind. These barriers may later become hedges, fences or tall trees. Use special symbols to record this information.

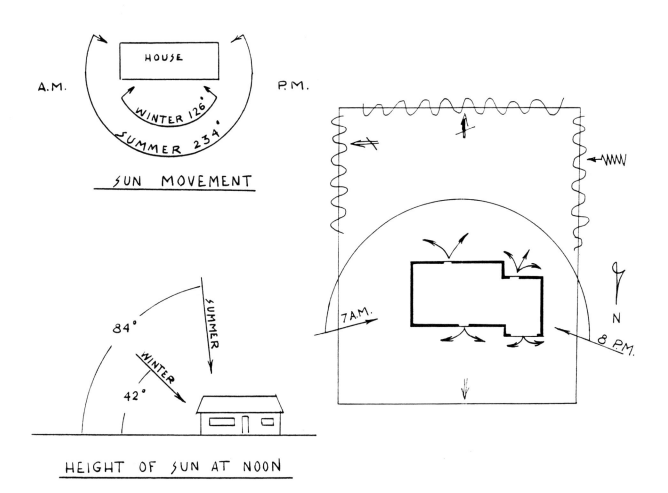

SUN MOVEMENT

HEIGHT OF SUN AT NOON

STEP 3—THE FUNCTION AREA PLAN

This plan is simple but important. Study the floor plan of your home and you will notice four distinct areas of usage: the public area where guests are usually seen (entry foyer, living room), the private area (bedrooms, bathrooms), the living area where recreation with family and friends takes place (family room), and the work area (kitchen, garage, laundry or utility room). Extend these areas into the landscape with large circles and inside each circle list those ideas you wish to use in that portion of the landscape. For example, the garden work area, vegetable garden, storage shed, and clothesline should be placed adjacent to the home work area.

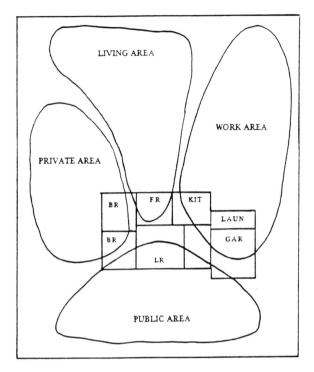

BASIC FUNCTION AREA PLAN

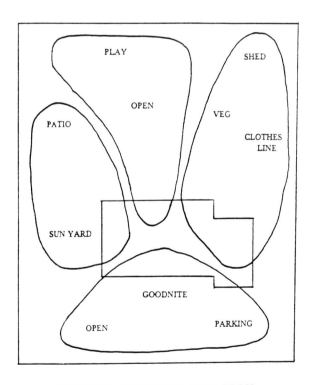

FINISHED FUNCTION AREA PLAN

STEP 4—THE PLANT BED DESIGN PLAN

Tape all of your plans onto a wall. Then, begin to sketch in the shapes of beds to hold the plants and constructions needed to provide the barriers between function areas. Make several sketches using strong flowing lines. Keep the design simple. Add shrub and tree forms at their full, mature size. Remember not to block foot-traffic flow. Plan for all plants to be in beds and use your finger to trace a path as you visualize a slow walk through the landscape. Scale is important on this drawing (1/8" = 1' is a good scale). Think in terms of plant shapes and heights, not plant names.

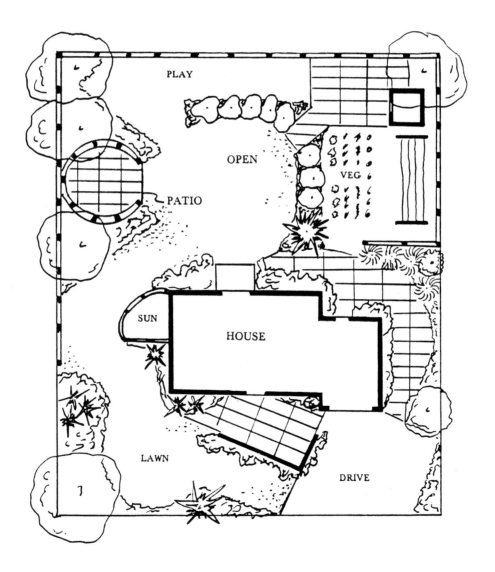

STEP 5—THE PLANTING PLAN

One additional plan is needed so your bed plan won't become crowded. This plan actually lists the quantity and names of all plants used and gives more detail about the construction items. Carefully study the plant lists in Chapter Seven for heights and state zones (N, C, or S). Most shrubs for mass barriers are planted three feet apart, most ground covers one to two feet apart. Consider the balance of color and texture, and remember that it is usually best to plant masses of single varieties in a bed rather than lots of individual species. Names and quantities can be listed in the plan or coded onto a table as shown here.

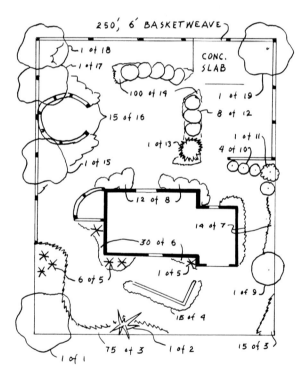

No.	QUAN	NAME
1	1	Silk Oak
2	1	Pfitzer Jun.
3	90	Shore Jun.
4	15	Dwarf Yaupon
5	7	Adam's Needle
6	30	Oyster Plant & Mulch
7	14	Kurume Azalea
8	12	Pittosporum, Var.
9	1	Loquat
10	4	Burford Holly
11	1	Ixora
12	8	Podocarpus
13	1	Red Cedar
14	100	Ajuga, Bronze
15	1	Tangerine
16	15	Croton
17	1	Mango
18	1	Orange
19	1	Jacaranda

Judge your landscape for usage

Once you've made your landscape plan on paper, walk around the landscape an hour or more noting where each landscape feature will be: trees, plant beds, benches, patio, foot paths, hedge or fence barriers. Then look for flaws and judge the usefulness of what you see. Does your landscape meet all the needs and desires of all the people who will use it? If not, go back to the drawing board. In this manner you will solve all your landscape problems *before* you invest hundreds of dollars in a landscape that might not be correct for your needs. Following is a list of considerations to help you make this judgment.

A. GOOD TRAFFIC CIRCULATION
  1. Are any obstacles (garbage cans, bicycles, shrubs) located where they might cause a hazard in the dark or create a mowing problem?
  2. Can movement be made around both sides of the home? Fenced rear yards should have at least two gates, preferably three.
  3. Is movement from car to entrance door made over a short, wide, hard surface?
  4. Is there easy movement to and from utilities (clothesline, tool shed, garbage cans)?

B. BARRIERS
  1. Are undesirable views, noise, wind, sun, garbage cans, clotheslines, small animals; children, and passersby completely or partially blocked out of particular landscape areas?
  2. Is privacy achieved in the private area of the landscape?

C. DISTINCT FUNCTION AREAS
  1. Is landscape effectively divided into distinct outdoor areas with suitable features to enjoy the designated functions?
    a. Public Area—well lighted with partial seclusion for greetings and good-byes.
    b. Private Area—enclosed or screened off to provide privacy for light entertaining, reading, snoozing.
    c. Play Area—somewhat isolated from other areas but viewable from kitchen or other much-used area of the house.
    d. Open Area—for sunbathing, yard games, viewing from patio or terrace.
    e. Work Area—isolated; may contain tool shed, clothesline, compost pile, vegetable garden, or service vehicle area.
  2. Are these areas separated by any barriers (fences, beds, hedges) or by changes of surface?

D. DRIVEWAY
  1. Is the driveway located away from play area or other areas of heavy foot traffic?
  2. Does the driveway lead near to the entrance door and is there easy accessibility to this area?
  3. Is it large enough to accommodate off-street parking for guests?
  4. Is off-street turnaround space available?
  5. Is a complete view of the sidewalk and street permitted when a car enters the street from the driveway?
  6. Does the driveway take up too much room on a small lot?

E. MAINTENANCE
  1. Does the landscape provide easy maintenance through the proper choice of plant materials?
  2. Is maintenance service provided or will you be providing maintenance?
  3. Is at least one family member horticulturally-minded to enjoy and maintain a high-maintenance landscape? If not, think *low-maintenance.*
  4. Is there too much grass? Too much edging? Are there too many shrubs to prune?

LIVING ROOM IN THE LAWN—Not a blade of grass can be seen in this outdoor living area that boasts two rooms divided by planters and different surface stones. The enclosure is lush tropical foliage backed by cypress fencing. The ceiling is picturesque live oaks.

Design: Robert Slatinsky—St. Petersburg

CANALSIDE DECK—A deck in this backyard doubles as a dock overhanging the seawall on a boat canal in Largo, Florida. The pilings support the dock as well as a permanent roof for shade and a sheltered feeling.

MULTIPURPOSE OUTDOOR ROOM—This useful privacy yard, separated from surrounding woods by a six-foot cypress fence, offers a hammock nap in a quiet corner, space for sunbathing, lots of hard surface from a deck of pressure-treated pine, seating for eight, a table for a lazy lunch, and no grass to mow. A highly usable living space.

Residence: Sue and Mike Clark

MINI-GARDEN—Landscape architect Joe Shaw has installed a seaside mini-garden containing lots of nuggets. Its features include: seating, a hard surface, a sea-pounded boulder, an edged and gravel-surfaced path, overhead lighting, and palm shade along with a host of colorful, low-maintenance ground covers.

Monty Trainer's Restaurant—Miami

TREEHOUSE DECK—Extending from a second-floor game room, this spacious deck at author's home comes complete with grill, fireplace, swinging chair, and eating room for six.

BAYOU VISTA—What a magnificent view of Long Bayou this rooftop patio affords. (You should see the sunsets.) To keep insects from entering the screened pool below, a screen cage was constructed at the top of the spiral steps leading down.

Design: Florian Hesse
Residence: Dr. & Mrs. Robert Burg—Seminole

A living picture (such as this coconut in a tropical setting) can be created if you design your landscape with a view from within.

CONVENIENT ENTRY—Antique bricks set in concrete form this circular drive that conveniently delivers guests to the front door. Residents use the drive (in foreground) that runs along the side of the house. In a few years these oaks will be large enough to create a majestic, shaded entrance drive.

MULTIPURPOSE DRIVE—This home was placed askew upon the lot to minimize the U-turn entrance to the garage. The large, free-formed drive provides off-street parking for six, has a convenient on-property turnaround to eliminate backing onto the main road, and is large enough for playing basketball, paddleball or badminton. See the tie-in between the flowing lines and the landscape beds?

Design: Mac Perry
Residence: Dr. & Mrs. Robert Burg

THE COUNTY SEAT—Some ideas never grow old. Unstained redwood wraps around the base of a stately tree to provide casual seating for eight. Notice the brick footing and surrounding flowers.

A PLANT HOSPITAL—A north-facing structure with corrugated fiberglass roof and back blocks any harsh winds and permits diffused light to reach ailing plants. Combine this with a mist system for maintaining 80% to 100% humidity and you have an excellent plant recuperation hospital. Notice the free access to natural air around the potted plants in this corner of the garden work center.

POOLSIDE BAR—Nestled in a corner just steps away from the blazing poolside sun is this Polynesian retreat cooled by a shadecloth roof. Landscape designer Ray Smith added reed fencing and *Ligustrum sinensis*, a cold-hardy but delicate-appearing, white-leafed shrub.

BENCH MADE TO BE SAT UPON—Few bench designers take the trouble to tilt the seat and back support to an angle which conforms to human comfort. This solid seat is very comfortable. And look how mud puddles are eliminated with the addition of a concrete base. Benches like this allow people to participate in the landscape—become a part of the living sculpture.

Design: Hefty's Heritage Backgrounds—St. Petersburg

A FULL DAY OF FUN—Some lucky kid is in heaven here. Climb the catwalk, run through the fort, slide down the fireman's pole or double slide out back. There's even a swing and a knotted rope to develop strength and dexterity. And for the little ones, a giant sandbox in the basement. From Wayne Hefty, a talented St. Petersburg designer of landscape constructions.

PLAYGROUND AT HOME—At the rear of the lot, in full view from the house, stands this child's activity center complete with a sandbox, fort, swing, Jacob's ladder, and monkey bars and sturdily constructed from pressure-treated pine and galvanized pipes.

SHADY LAKESIDE RETREAT—Tucked under the shade of a grove of wax myrtles (*Myrica cerifera*), this handsome deck affords a pleasant view of a peaceful lake in Dunedin. There are night lights, seats, and lots of room for a late evening picnic thanks to the talents of designer Wayne Hefty. Note that the trees grew through the holes in the deck (just kidding).

GARDEN IN A BOX—One view of this side-yard vegetable garden shows wood frame vegetable boxes with attached wire fencing (to keep out rodents). The boxes are filled with a mixture of leaves, grass clippings, and peat—then sterilized once a year with Vapam to keep out root-feeding nematodes. Note the abundance of storage space in the well-camouflaged sheds.

ANOTHER VIEW reveals the lattice-covered patio that allows the grower to sit in the shade and simply watch the plants grow.
Residence: Sue and Mike Clark

POTTING SHED—In the midst of a garden, surrounded by a dense clump of bananas and native cabbage palms, a spacious work center offers an area where young seedlings and cuttings can be potted and placed under mist for a few weeks before moving them into the garden.

Residence: Mr. and Mrs. Harold C. Anderson

THOUGHTLESS NEIGHBOR SYNDROME—The deeds of a thoughtless neighbor who stacks his lumber in view of this home-owner's landscape are quickly snuffed out by a few short sections of basketweave cypress fence. The arborvitaes will soon grow and cover the abrupt end posts to soften this focal point as seen from the Florida room.

Residence: Mike Falkingham, Largo

A QUIET CORNER—An inexpensive reed fence surrounds this pocket at the rear of the landscape to insure peace and solitude. The bench is a simple concrete slab set upon blocks on a ground cover of gravel—a quiet retreat from a busy summer afternoon. Shade is provided by a Brazilian pepper tree (*Schinus terebinthifolius*), often considered pesty because of its rapid, sprawling growth. The prickly plants are Spanish bayonet (*Yucca alotifolia*).

ROUTE TO THE REAR—Access to the backyard is provided by the lawn itself as it wedges between two thickly planted beds.

PLANT BED SHORTCUT—Both vertical and horizontal railroad ties support this raised bed that swings out into the lawn to soften and extend the corner of the home. And if you look closely you'll see a step and a path cutting across the bed to provide a shortcut to the rear yard.

A TENDER TRAIL TO SOMEWHERE—You may find paths made of brick, block, and wood, but it's hard to beat the tender simplicity of one carved from the lawn itself. This one is lined with spider plants (*Chlorophytum comosum*) and feathery springeri fern (*Asparagus sprengeri*).

ENERGY SAVER—Huge elms (*Ulmus* spp.), planted to the west side of this handsome home of Joe and Elsie Lang of St. Petersburg, shed their leaves in the winter to permit the sun to warm the house before nightfall. In summer the leaves shade and cool the house.

LANDSCAPE MADE FOR BUSY GARDENERS

The home of Mr. and Mrs. Ronald Prince of St. Petersburg is set in a highly functional landscape developed especially for their active gardening lifestyle. Over the years the Princes have added and added until now every usable space is filled with growing things.

WAIST-HIGH STRAWBERRIES—You never have to bend over to pick these strawberries. The Princes use every available space by planting in attractive, tiered troughs along a back fence of their landscape. The flowers beneath the troughs catch the excess fertilizer and water.

CORNER FOR GROWING—The Princes use the extra space at the side of their house for growing lettuce in gutters tiered up a south-facing wall. Several basket hangers support plants waiting to reach maturity when they will be moved to a more desirable location. Popcorn stepping-stones direct foot traffic onto a patch of lawn reserved for sunning and hanging laundry to air-dry.

GARDEN IN A BOX—Ten-year-old Clay Perry (the author's son) waters vegetables at a local school where students learn about plant growth. Plants are growing in a frame of leaves and grass clippings. Gro-Boxes like this make neat gardens for roses, annuals, cut flowers, or vegetables. If you can offer your time to help with a project like this, I'll bet your local school district will accept it, and I'll bet you'll enrich many children's lives.

DRESSING A FENCE—At the far end of the landscape, another patch of lawn, a rich bed of flowers, and hanging baskets provide a pleasant vista and mini bird sanctuary.

GARDENER'S POTTING BENCH—At the exit side of the landscape a solid potting bench made from pressure-treated pine covers a series of plastic garbage cans containing peat moss, sand, potting soil and fertilizer. Notice the convenience of running water and extra fire-wood storage.

GRO-BOX GARDENING—Dominating the rest of the rear yard are Gro-Boxes for the family vegetables. Raised gardens keep foot traffic from compacting the soil, allow excess water to drain away, and make attractive working units for propagating, germinating seedlings, or growing vegetables. Note attractive compost box in back corner.

Don'ts in the landscape

DON'T . . . plant large plants in front of your front door and smaller plants to the side. Use the "funnel effect" that will draw attention down to the front door, the eye of the home. Also DON'T:

—water lawn daily. It produces a shallow-rooted lawn.
—use black plastic to keep out weeds. It causes watering problems.
—overuse white gravel in landscape beds. It's glaring.
—plant sharp-pointed plants near doors or traffic areas.
—plant deciduous shrubs near the front door. They're bare in winter.
—plant short bloom-season plants in conspicuous places near the front door.
—plant perennials in the vegetable garden because you'll need to sterilize bare soil occasionally to prevent nematode damage.
—water tops of shrubs. This spreads disease.
—spray lawn weeds with herbicides in the hot sum-mer. This could burn the grass.
—space plants so that the bed looks full when new. It will get too crowded later.
—plant Punk or Ficus near the driveway or foundation as they will uproot concrete.
—plant trees over a sewer line. The roots will clog the sewer.
—plant trees under utility cables (TV, telephone, electric).
—plant thick shrubs near a driveway where you block the view of cars backing onto a thoroughfare.
—install only one gate in a fence around the backyard. Put in three.
—place beds in natural paths of foot-traffic.
—let rain uproot your plants under the roof line. Use gutters.
—include fish ponds, bird baths and feeders, etc., in your landscape unless you have the time, desire, and knowledge to care for them.

Don't . . . plant trees like Cuban laurel and Punk whose anchor roots grow on top of the lawn to create a mowing problem and mower blade hazard.

DON'T

Don't . . . install fencing close to drive. It will scratch your car door and cramp your usable drive space. Keep fences at least three feet away.

DON'T

Don't . . . underestimate the growing power of *Arborvitae*. They will dwarf your home and hide its beauty. Like baby alligators, they won't stay small and cute very long.

DON'T

Don't . . . plant several trees in the open lawn. It creates mowing and edging problems and, often, tree trunks get torn and scarred by the mower or weed eater, leaving them susceptible to disease. Wrap a plant bed around these trees—much more visually interesting as well as practical.

DON'T

Don't . . . team up with your neighbors to replace grass with gravel. The weeds still come through and the effect of a gravel lawn is hot and unpleasing to the eye.

DON'T

Plants with extensive root systems such as those in the Ficus family should never be planted in raised planters or in confined landscape spaces.

C H A P T E R

Two

EARLY MORNING REFLECTION—Emotional excitement is created by the morning sun mirroring this multi-trunk shade tree set upon a dew-glistening lawn. Plant beds surround this living sculpture to show it off.

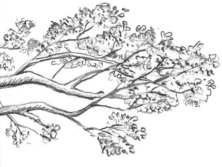

How to make your landscape beautiful

After you have determined those features which will make your landscape functional, the next step is to arrange these plants and construction features into a balanced, visually appealing design. This is done on paper. It is much cheaper to rearrange plants on paper than it is to redig them.

Often designers will make many sketches, rearranging the features, regrouping and changing, until they have a design solution that is not only functional but enjoyable to view. A landscape is like a living sculpture with people at its center. How much the people enjoy their landscape, both functionally and aesthetically, determines the success of a particular design solution.

Beauty, whether in a landscape or a poem, a symphony or a painting, must excite emotion. There are certain principles of design that all artists use in order to excite emotion. The paradigm of these principles (rhythm, contrast, textures, line, focalization, harmony, form, etc.) can be summarized in what I call "UBS"—which stands for unity, balance, and simplicity.

There is beauty in unity. Do all the plants and construction features blend to make one unified statement? Is this garden primarily formal or informal? Is there a consistent theme—Polynesian, Japanese, tropical? Do the stones, wood, and concrete in the landscape match those of the house and surrounding areas to give harmony to the whole landscape?

There is beauty in balance. Is there good proportion between planted areas and open green areas, plants and construction features? Is there a stable balance of color and texture in the foliage? Are the plants scaled to match the size of the house and lot? Has a conscious decision been made regarding symmetry and asymmetry? Either works as a basic design but consistency looks best.

And there is beauty in simplicity. Have long hedges or blank walls been accented with plants? Is there a single focal point at a distant corner of the landscape? Are the beds massed with single varieties of plants? Do the shapes and placement of the landscaped beds flow in a simple rhythmic curve?

Look now to see how landscape designers use UBS to establish beauty in our midst.

A mobile home lot can be landscaped for a plant collector's nature trail

The rear patio is hard surfaced for low maintenance and family barbeques. A winding trail leads through an arrangement of boulders, ground covers and specimen plants collected by the owners to a bench at the rear of the property. The trail can be naturalized with leaves or pine needles, sodded or made from river gravel (kept weed-free with a sheet of black plastic under it).

Avoid tension from your landscape

Always design with the mature size of your shrubs and trees in mind. Study the style and size of the home carefully. Don't let your plants detract from the home itself. Landscape plants should complement the home, not compete with it. Here are three common errors seen in thoughtless landscapes.

RESTLESS

SQUEEZED

OVERPOWERED

Train espalier in different patterns

U

DOUBLE U

FAN

Espalier is a plant that has been trained in a geometric plane. The U pattern and double U (or candelabra) were the original patterns used by early growers of dooryard fruit. These patterns facilitate picking and pruning and make an attractive design. For shapes like the fan, plantings of almost any tall-growing, small-leafed shrub can be used. Pyracantha and creeping fig (*Ficus pumila*) are very popular. Sometimes strings or wooden lattices are used for a diamond pattern. One rooted cutting of creeping fig at the base of each string does the trick. Periodic trimming is important.

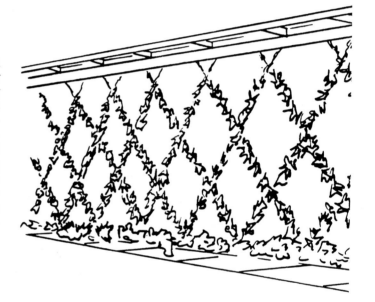

Make a topiary in one afternoon

Most topiaries are grown in the ground and shaped over a period of several years. But this technique utilizes galvanized wire to shape animals, lollipops, and other subjects. Stuff the finished wire forms with damp sphagnum moss. Then insert rooted cuttings of creeping fig vine (*Ficus pumila*) into the moss. The final topiary is portable and is best watered by soaking the figure in a tub of water containing a small amount of soluble fertilizer available from garden supply stores.

Landscape a cul-de-sac pool home for beauty

A heavily landscaped drive opens onto a spacious entry patio that leads to the front door or onto a flowing enclosed front yard. Notice it is the shape of the lawn that is pleasing, not the shape of the beds. From the rear lawn you have three options: enter the hidden shed area, step up to the raised deck, or enter the pool area. Low-maintenance shrubbery and minimum lawn area result in minimum landscape upkeep.

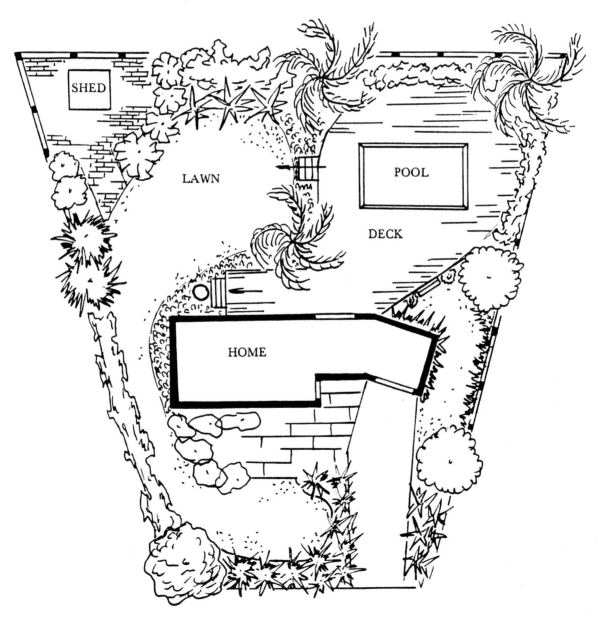

Make a broad one-story home appear taller on a narrow lot

This design technique utilizes a trick of the trade. Broad houses appear broader when horizontal lines made by the roof are exposed and vertical lines made by the walls are blocked from view. Simply reverse the order by locating plants that break the horizontal lines and expose the vertical ones. The opposite procedure can be used when you have a tall house you want to appear wider.

STUNNING BORDER DISPLAY—For a spectacular attraction, plant varying heights and colors of caladium tubers along a border. Edging plant is *Liriope muscari*.

FOOTBALL STADIUM EFFECT—Low, green *Liriope* are backed by silver dusty miller, then red-leafed copper plants—all within the backdrop of a taller hedgerow to produce a sweeping effect much like that of a football stadium.

TYING THE PLANT BED TO THE WALL—The large stones in the corner wall of this home seem to leave the wall and flow into the landscape giving the plant bed the same solidity as the architectural structure itself, harmonizing the two. Blue-vase junipers surround a *Ligustrum lucidum* tree.

RHYTHM AND BLUES—With heavenly blue skies for a backdrop this bed of *Pittosporum tobira* seems to march along with an endless rhythm of the ages. Can you see why?

JOHNNY COMES MARCHING HOME—Looking for ideas to create rhythm in your landscape? Check out this one from the rhythmic mind of Clearwater landscape architect, William H. Roy. Hup, two, three, four.

A FOCAL POINT WITH PULL POWER—A focal point may be a simple bench framed by *Cocos plumosa* palms set at some distant point from the patio or Florida room. See how those huge circular stones dance you away from the house and into the landscape?

RHYTHM IN THE ROUND—Giant stepping-stones resound the simple, circular pattern of the two beds at the front of the house. Plopped between two driveways, they gesture an invitation to your next-door neighbor.

Design: William H. Roy, landscape architect, Clearwater

WOODSY SCENE—Northern landscapers working near Jacksonville in more rural, wooded locations like to utilize the natural elements. Here the lawn is separated from naturally balanced woodside growth by low shrubbery and a few large boulders. Add a little snow and we have the makings of a Christmas card.

American Association of Nurserymen

THREE PLANES OF ACTION—First the eyes stop on the nearby bed of shore juniper (*Juniperus conferta*) with a framing palm trunk. Then they move to the mid-range cluster of pygmy date palms (*Phoenix roebelenii*) that introduce the house. They finally come to rest at the distant cluster of shrubs and tall Eucalyptus that stop the visual flow. These three planes give depth to this well-designed driveway.

WHERE STRAIGHT LINES WORK—Like a platoon of Confederate soldiers at attention, these rigid Southern cedars (*Juniperus silicicola*) uniformly guard a colonial brick wall. The straight plant bed repeats the line of the wall to emphasize the structured formality. No flow here; it wouldn't fit this strict unity.

ADORNING A FENCE—An assortment of flowering vines casually conceals a cypress rail fence reminiscent of "down on the farm." The first is *Lantana montevidensis*, the second *Allamanda violacea*. For a full list of vines for your landscape, see the chart in Chapter Seven.

EYE-APPEAL HOLLIES—Carefully pruned yaupon hollies (*Ilex vomitoria*) cluster around the base of a Jerusalem thorn (*Parkinsonia aculeata*) to provide eye appeal. Who wouldn't give this scene a second look?

COURTYARD PATIO HAS IT ALL—See how this Membership Garden at St. Petersburg's Museum of Fine Arts achieves a high level of aesthetic enjoyment by adhering to so many of the principles of design: an ever-changing play of shadows on the wall; the scaled-down shrubbery; a fountain as the focal point; visual accent from garden art (The Praying Boy); the rhythmic flow of the plant beds; the texture of the brick floor; mushroom lights for evening enjoyment; trickling water to appeal to the sense of sound; shelter from a single, large tree; depth from three planes of plantings; variety; proportion—the list goes on. Careful planning makes gardens like this a success.

FRAMING AND FOCALIZATION—See how these angled *Cocos plumosa* palms provide a frame for the pool area? The purple leaf ground cover is oyster plant (*Rheo discolor*). The distant planter of *Phoenix roebelenii* palms becomes a focal point.

THE OLD SWIMMING HOLE—This handsome pool was constructed in what appears to be a forest but is actually the heavily planted backyard of Jim and Marge Mang of Largo.

STEADY FLOW, FRONT TO REAR—Like playful elves, close-cropped hollies (*Ilex vomitoria*) dance around the base of this handsome home. See how they carry you from the front yard to the back without a break in the flow of the landscape?

Residence of Mr. & Mrs. Gary N. Strohauer, Seminole

CYPRESS ENTRY ARCH—Tall Italian cypresses (*Cupressus sempervirens*) are pulled over and tied to form an entry arch to frame this front yard. The trunk of the close-cropped Cuban laurel (*Ficus retusa* "Nitida") is stuffed with spider plants and an assortment of flowers.

Residence of Mr. & Mrs. Charles Byrd, St. Petersburg

SIMPLY BEAUTIFUL—Simplicity is maintained by planting only one species of flowers in this large bed. Brilliant petunias will bloom all fall, winter, and spring. Palms are the once misnamed *Cocos plumosa* now called *Syagrus romanzoffianum*.

DRIVEWAY WITH RHYTHM—Like giant darts from outer space, three live oaks pierce the center of this huge drive in a rhythmic pattern that disrupts the monotony of all that concrete. Can you feel the rhythm—bong, bong, bong?

STATELY PALMS ACCENT—A majestic clump of *Phoenix reclinata* frames and shelters this Florida home.

TWO-STORY TREES—Two-story houses require two-story palms if they are to provide adequate scale for the house. Here a framing cluster of *Cocos plumosa* is used so the house won't be overpowering. Juniper ground cover is punctuated by a specimen king sago palm (*Cycas revoluta*).

TREE FOR SHELTER—Famed landscape architect Garrett Eckbo talks about the floors, walls, and ceiling of a landscape. When your landscape has a ceiling like this large camphor tree (*Cinnamomum camphora*), physical and psychological comfort are evident without blocking view. The cascading ground cover is low-maintenance springeri fern(*Asparagus sprengeri*) which becomes the walls. The floor is a solid trip-free deck.

American Association of Nurserymen

THE GREAT ALUMINUM COVERUP—Mobile homes often have skinny, metallic arms that dangle from the edge of their aluminum cabana roofs. Clothe these arms in the softness and permanence of Confederate jasmine (*Trachelospermum jasminoides*). The framing formal trees are Norfolk Island pines (*Araucaria excelsa*).

GOOD ADVICE?—"Leave it alone and it will landscape itself." That's one school of thought. But remember it doesn't always work as well as this example. Here nature's planting of wild muscadine grapes grows over a country driveway near Lake Wales. This is about as informal as you can get. But you can duplicate it with cultivated species grown on a fence and arched trellis.

SIMPLY NEAT—Crisply edged grass with mulch, low trimmed *Ilex vomitoria*, and giant *Liriope muscari* create a neat and simple edging for live oaks.

LANDSCAPE FOR ALL THE SENSES

Beauty in the landscape is a pleasing quality that arouses a contemplative delight and is brought about through an aesthetic excitation of the senses—all the senses. Many homeowners make the common mistake of designing a site to appeal to the sense of sight only.

A landscape that appeals to sight, sound, touch, smell and taste will be more greatly appreciated, loved, and used by those who dwell within it. And remember, landscapes are for people.

Here are some examples of landscapes that are designed to appeal to all the senses.

SEE THE LANDSCAPE—Yellow is one of the boldest colors in the landscape. It can be seen for blocks. And the largest of the yellows is produced by this *Allamanda cathartica*. See Chapter Seven for a thorough list of showy plants.

HEAR THE LANDSCAPE—Rugged boulders surround this noisy, trickling, splashing, cascading, recirculating river pool alongside Monty Trainer's restaurant on Biscayne Bay in Miami. Ferns and geraniums grow in pockets formed by the stones. The wall on the left is faced with creeping fig vines and reed-appearing galingale plants (*Cyperus* spp.).

DESIGN: Joe Shaw, Landscape Architect

TOUCH THE LANDSCAPE—Some trees like this birch (*Betula populifolia*) gracing a Pensacola pond draw viewers to touch their interesting bark. Other bark lures include punk, sycamore, and pine. The sense of touch is further excited by comfortable benches, solid walks, soft lawn and touchable annuals like *celosia*.

TASTE THE LANDSCAPE—Dozens of fruit varieties are available to Florida residents including our champion orange seen here. Notice how competitive grasses are kept out by heavy mulching of cypress bark.

SMELL THE LANDSCAPE—The fragrance of springtime comes alive in *Wisteria sinensis* planted at the base of this north Florida pine trunk. Other plants offering a sweet scent include gardenia, night-blooming jasmine, sweet viburnum, citrus, roses, and angel's trumpet.

INTERIORSCAPE—A skylight high above provides plenty of light for the abundant foliage of the trailing Philodendron and for the potted plants below.

Hughes Homes

EDEN OASIS—A furnished patio rests next to a swirling spa whose waters spill over smooth, flat stones to a refreshing pool below. The trickling sound and screened enclosure replete with potted foliage make this a garden paradise.

Hughes Homes

A SIMPLE RHYTHM—A brick path meanders from the sidewalk through a soft Bermuda grass lawn. Rhythmic flow is created by the curving path and the circular beds highlighted in white limerock. Framing palms are *Sabal palmetto*, Florida's state tree.

NATURAL BEAUTY—This mini-forest clustered with an assortment of plants is isolated from the walkway and closely clipped grass by stacked landscape timbers. In this manner a segment of the natural world is brought into a manicured landscape.

A NATURAL LANDSCAPE—Native saw palmettos were left to form a well-textured border for this side yard in Jacksonville. Notice how a sod path provides passage to the play yard.

BEAUTIFUL DRIVE ECHOES HOUSE TEXTURE—When it comes to driveways, who can dispute the beautiful texture of these bomonite blocks. See how they harmonize with the pattern in the siding and window panes of this handsome colonial-style home? Huge orange trees make this a real Southern homestead complete with Southern bench and Confederate cannon.

DAZZLING PETUNIAS—Stunning white petunias flow along this lawn to afford a spectacular explosion of color from the lawn or pool area. White flowers can be seen from a greater distance than any other color.

HARMONY VS. CONTRAST—There is harmony in the similar textures of the tiny foliage of the shore juniper ground cover, the pittosporum shrub, and the laurel oak tree. But it is set in contrast by the changes in the colors from dark to light to dark again. Just as there is harmony in the texture of the brick wall but contrast in its ever-changing colors. And the whole scene is set behind a flowing line that separates all the textural action from the peaceful stillness of the soft, green lawn. It is unified, balanced, and simplified—UBS.

Residence: Mr. and Mrs. Michael Kashtan, Seminole

Japanese Gardens

Due to the scarcity of garden space in Japan, intensely cultivated gardens have evolved over the centuries. All prominent families as well as inns, restaurants, and historic mansions maintain elaborate gardens. These are usually secluded behind tall fences or dense plantings which prevent their being seen from the street.

The first view of a typical Japanese garden comes from inside the house, from the zashiki, the all-purpose principal room. From here, most of the main garden is portrayed. But often there are other gardens: an entrance garden, an inner garden, a tea garden. The passage through a tea garden to the tea house is a part of the tea ceremony itself. The landscape here is designed with such simplicity as to separate participants emotionally from the outside world in preparation for the tea ceremony.

In the development of a Japanese garden two factors are important: first, to incorporate a distant view, "borrowed scenery," through some hole in the landscape; second, to utilize natural features as much as possible.

Nature is the major influence in a Japanese garden. Often, sections of the garden are reminiscent of a forest, a coastline, or the universe itself. These gardens are prepared using three elements—stone, water, and plants—arranged so as to portray a glimpse of nature and depict humanity's place in it.

Stone, sand, and boulders are used liberally in Japanese gardens. Boulders are used as retaining walls to hold soil, as borders for a dry streambed, and to represent islands in an ocean of raked sand suggesting the waves of the sea.

Smaller stones are used for paths or to simulate a river flow. Flat stones are often used as stepping-stones across a wet or dry stream.

Water features may be wet or dry (simulated with stone) as long as the presence of water is felt. Real water from a waterfall or splashing over stones gives the added joy of sound in the landscape.

Streams should meander back and forth, their borders studded with stones, wood, or plants, and spill into an irregularly shaped pond.

Plants in a Japanese garden are often of a small-leafed variety. Florida gardeners should use lots of needle evergreens like pines, junipers, cedar. Also yaupon holly (*Ilex vomitoria*), azaleas, dogwood, maple, plum, saucer magnolia, bamboo, papyrus, redbud, mondo grass, mimosa, fern, and moss can be used. Bright, colorful flowers should generally be avoided.

Many of the shrubs can be shaped into pompom-like balls to resemble clouds. Japanese gardeners trim their plants to their own liking, pinching pine candles in the spring and shaping azaleas to spread close to the ground or to cascade over a boulder.

Bamboo of all types is used: smaller ones near a stream, larger ones to provide shelter and backdrop enclosure. Bamboo features are common as fences, gates, torch holders, or pipes for delivering water to a basin.

Bonsai also is common. These miniature trees living in the shallow of soil require much maintenance in the Japanese garden. Most trees are under two feet tall and are scaled-down versions of age-old forest giants.

Other ornaments of the Japanese garden include an assortment of lanterns, water basins, pagodas, curved and flat footbridges, and noisemakers made of bamboo.

Following are a few ideas you may want to incorporate into your Japanese garden.

A SEASCAPE—Japanese landscape gardeners cover bare ground with gravel, often raked to depict waves, to represent the universal sea. Carefully selected boulders emerge as mountainous islands.

STONE LANTERNS—Originally tea masters borrowed dedication lanterns from old temples and shrines to decorate their tea gardens. Today lanterns are commonplace and no Japanese garden should be without one. These lanterns are made of carved or molded stone pieces and can be placed anywhere in the garden as an ornament.

BAMBOO FENCING—An excellent Oriental fence can be constructed of tied bamboo to add a Japanese flavor to the garden.

JAPANESE SEAT—A thick, flat stone resting upon huge, rough timbers placed on gravel under a sheltering tree suggests the mass and balance of the earth at rest.

JAPANESE FOOTBRIDGE—Japanese gardens frequently use water, rocks, aquatic plants and a small, arched footbridge embellished (but not supported) by bamboo. This one is seen at Walt Disney World's Epcot Center near Orlando.

JAPANESE MINIATURES—Across the distant sea (pea gravel) emerge strong islands (boulders) backed by a forest of greenery. Japanese landscapes are miniatures of their own coastlines. The lacy framing tree in the foreground is a Chinese tallow (*Sapium sebiferum*).

Bamboo

Bamboo has its own special place in Japanese and Polynesian gardens. The word bamboo refers to a group of tall, evergreen, ornamental grasses found under an assortment of botanical names including *Arundinaria*, *Bambusa*, *Pseudosasa*, and *Phyllostachys*. They grow best in moist, heavy loam soils and prefer a little shade over full sun. Bamboo is easily propagated by separating a clump with a shovel and planting individual plants elsewhere.

Don't place bamboo plants in too conspicuous a location as they tend to look a little shabby in the spring following a cold winter. As their tops begin to brown, prune them by cutting the entire cane at ground level. New canes come up from the root system.

Give bamboo plenty of room to spread but don't let it get out of hand. The larger varieties make excellent backgrounds to enclose your garden. Use smaller varieties in central areas and clumping varieties for special effects.

CHINESE GODDESS BAMBOO (*Bambusa* spp.)—If a cluster effect is desired, this variety is one of the best. Note the lengths of giant timber bamboo (*Phyllostachys bambusoides*) being used as a fence in the foreground.

GIANT TIMBER BAMBOO (*Phyllostachys bambusoides*)—This Japanese bamboo grows to 70 feet in height and five inches in diameter. Its shoots are edible and its large trunk is used in construction of houses, fences, and walls. These young ones will need thinning out as they mature. Caution: After a rare winter freeze, you may have giant dead bamboo to cut and dispose of.

FEMALE ARROW BAMBOO (*Pseudosasa japonica*)—This species is a smaller-growing variety that grows well in heavy shade.

MINIATURE BAMBOO—One of the smallest varieties is this one called switchcans (*Arundinaria tecta*). It provides an eye-level bamboo for small gardens.

Bonsai—Nature in Miniature

Bonsai, an ancient Chinese art adapted by the Japanese and introduced on the U.S. West Coast after World War II, is a product of garden art under the pressure of limited space. Florida bonsai hobbyists strive to wire and train trees to grow in small shallow pots, the soil of which is covered with moss, miniature boulders, and dwarf flowers to depict nature in miniature. The object is to scale down the trunk, limbs, and leaves to duplicate closely a large tree that has braved the elements of nature and persevered in time. Like most Japanese art forms, bonsai is nature in miniature. Some of these tiny "tray plants," which require daily watering and careful maintenance, are passed from generation to generation and long outlive their first planter. The word "ming tree" usually refers to a plastic version or a larger sculptured topiary shrub in the landscape and should not be applied to a live bonsai growing in a shallow dish.

BONSAI MINIATURE TREE—Aerial roots from a *Ficus benjamina* add age and character to this bonsai grown by Cecil Wise of Seminole.

WINDSWEPT BONSAI—A cliff-dwelling, cascade appearance gives this thick-trunked *Juniperus procumbens* bonsai its aesthetic value. Pot is traditional bonsai type with drain holes, tiny feet, and unglazed inside. Evergreens are popular for bonsai because of their tiny leaves.

AGED BONSAI—Over 100 years old, this Trident Maple grows in a mere two-inch tray. This "most handsome bonsai in the world" displays miniature leaves and a massive, gnarled trunk reminiscent of its prototype. It provides a real inspiration for hobbyists who like this ancient Japanese horticultural art.

BONSAI STARTS—A wide variety of shrubs and trees being trained as bonsai, dwarf Japanese trees.

Polynesian Gardens

Like Japanese gardens, Polynesian gardens take their character from the countryside and traditions of the land of their origin. In Polynesia—from islands in the south Pacific to Hawaii—the climate is hot, humid, and tropical. Polynesian gardens are characterized by the use of palm fronds to form the walls and rooftops of open shelters, called tiki huts (after Tiki, a traditional Polynesian god), bamboo to hold torches for night lighting, and an assortment of sculptured gods and goddesses carved from the trunks of palm trees.

Grass skirts and leis made of bright, colorful flowers represent unique uses of landscape plants. In Polynesian countries many large, tropical and colorfully flowering shrubs and trees are grown. The flowers are used to adorn the hair, clothing, and the home. Seeds and seed pods are used to make necklaces and musical instruments.

Florida more than any other state has the closest climate to that of Polynesia. For a Polynesian garden in Florida, try growing colorful plants such as frangipani (a common lei flower), anthurium, billbergia, pineapple, croton, poinsettia, heleconia, Jerusalem thorn, orchid tree, royal poinciana, bougainvillea, bird of paradise, and oleander. Most any colorful flowering plant will do. And, for excitement, be sure to hang a collection of orchids from the limbs of your trees.

A SUNKEN PATIO—A Polynesian god carved from a palm log glares through a pair of *Phoenix roebelenii* palms in this attractive sunken garden, situated in full view of, yet safely distant from splashing from the adjacent pool.

Design: Robert Slatinsky, St. Petersburg

DISTINCTLY POLYNESIAN—Imagine trade winds rustling the thatched roof of the folded and dried cabbage palm fronds (*Sabal palmetto*) of this tiki bar. Have a luau, light the torch or build a fire. All kinds of recreational uses are possible. Listen for the sound of a distant drum. Hula . . . hula, Polynesia.

BAMBOO TORCH—Night torches, so typical in Polynesian gardens, are made decorative when encased within the slats of a sliced giant timber bamboo.

SCULPTURED DEITY—Polynesian gods can be carved from old logs and painted or stained for an accent piece in your Polynesian garden.

Tiki Gardens, Indian Shores

POTTING BENCH WITH A THEME—In the Polynesian garden of the author's home, giant timber bamboo were cut into four-foot lengths and placed loosely in a frame facing a potting bench. Broad planking on top doubles as an hors d'oeuvres counter at luau time. The ground cover is billbergia with brilliant red flower heads.

HAWAIIAN HOVEL—Folded and dried cabbage palm fronds (on a simple frame wall) and slats of cypress (on the roof) transform a children's playhouse (or storage shed) to blend into any Polynesian landscape. Pour a concrete slab floor first or for dry surface "loose set" square stepping-stones on sand.

Tiki Gardens, Indian Shores

Living Art

Garden art utilizing plants comes in many forms: dried flower arrangements, cut floral arrangements, clipped hedges of assorted shapes, and more. Among the most popular are the shaping arts, espalier and topiary.

Espalier is a simple technique in which a tree or shrub is trained on a trellis or against a flat wall so that the trunk and branches all lie in one plane (giving it height and width but no depth); in other words, a mature espalier is a two-dimensional sculptured plant.

The term is used both as a verb to describe the technique and as a noun referring to the plant itself. It is pronounced es-pal´-yer.

Traditionally espaliers were fruit trees trained like candelabra to facilitate harvesting and take up less space. But today, in Florida, with the exception of grapes, espaliers are grown for ornamental purposes.

Pyracantha is a favorite choice, but almost any plant can be used—magnolia, viburnum, clusia, podocarpus. Judicious pruning may be necessary to force the plant to grow in designated sites. And usually nails of some type and insulated wire are necessary to hold limbs in position.

Topiary differs from espalier in that it is three-dimensional instead of two. Topiary has been called sculptured shrubbery. It may be small (puff clouds along a creek bank carved out of yaupon holly) or large (the giant animated figures on the lawn at Walt Disney World).

Topiary technique works best with simple shapes. The choice of plant for trimming should be one with relatively dense foliage, able to retain its leaves year-round and to hold foliage close to the ground.

Perhaps the best choice for growth in Florida is one of the podocarpus varieties. Other choices include viburnum, ligustrum, yaupon holly, and for larger specimens, weeping fig and Cuban laurel. Any dense, small-leafed shrub will do.

Topiary shapes may be formal such as tiered lollipops or inverted cones, or they may be informal, such as asymmetrical trees or the cloud shapes found in Japanese gardens.

Perhaps the largest and most diversified array of topiary in Florida is located at Walt Disney World. On spacious grounds near the Contemporary Hotel can be seen giant serpents swimming through the turf, a daisy chain of elephants, and the favorite of all, Mary Poppins.

These figures are trained and grown in huge tubs for many months at the Walt Disney World nursery nearby. When ready they are transported and transplanted into the grounds. The biggest problem is getting leaves to grow on the undersides of elephant tummies and other shaded locations on the giant figures. (As a solution, I'd suggest placing reflective shields under the figures, to cast the sun upward and force out new leaves. But, then, no one asked me.) The Disney solution is to replace fallen leaves with plastic, artificial leaves—an old Hollywood trick.

INVERTED PYRAMID—Checkerboard designs like this are among the most difficult to create and maintain. All growth comes from one plant, *Pyracantha coccinea*.

Office of Wm. J. Bone, D.V.M., Seminole

THE CANDELABRA—Candlestick design espaliers are the most popular. Pyracantha is a vigorous grower and will produce this shape in two to three years but must be pruned often to keep its shape.

PYRACANTHA ESPALIER—Espalier, the two-dimensional landscape art, works best against a span of blank wall. The pattern might be formal, free-flowing, or even the initials of a sweetheart. Underlining this pyracantha are springeri ferns.

Residence of Mr. & Mrs. Anan Savetemal, Largo

FULL-SCALE ESPALIER—Congratulations to this energetic homeowner in Gainesville for producing a two-story espalier from the tree *Magnolia grandiflora*.

SEA GRAPE ESPALIER—Artistically arrayed on this roadside facade in South Miami is a splendid espaliered row of large-leaf sea grapes.

GRANDIOSE HEDGE—Towering two stories tall at the border of this and other Palm Beach homes is a majestic hedgerow of Cuban laurels. These closely cropped giants become organic extensions of the homes and are unique to Florida's famed Atlantic coast.

TEXTURED VISTA—At Parrot Jungle on Miami's southside, giant A*gave* spp. display spiny texture in contrast to the soft green turf. Because these leaf tips are sharp as swords, plant A*gave* in distant vistas where they can be seen but not touched.

ROCK GARDEN—Terracing is common with rock garden enthusiasts. This one displays a vast collection of cacti as well as *Haworthia*, *Aloe*, *Sedum*, and pineapple. The environment provides good drainage, full sun, and protection from freeze.

At residence of Mr. and Mrs. Harold C. Anderson, St. Petersburg

EYE-HIGH HERBS—Handsome Florida cypress planter boxes tiered up a wall bring culinary herbs within an arm's reach of the patio chef. In Florida, herbs can be grown year-round.

Residence: Sue and Mike Clark

Formal Gardens

The formal garden probably had its origin in the early Egyptian empire whose agronomists out of necessity dug canals from the Nile River to bring water into their dry land. Fruit and vegetable crops were grown along the banks in linear, symmetrical arrangements.

Early Egyptians planted even more elaborate gardens near their homes and sacred buildings so they could wander in the shade amongst the trees and fragrant flowers.

The concept of symmetry in garden design later influenced the Greek city garden and the Roman country villa garden, called "topiarius" because of its formal, clipped hedges.

During the subsequent Dark Ages monks who preserved books and other early art forms also cultivated formal gardens inside their monastery walls or "horts"—thus "horticulture" was born.

With the fifteenth-century awakening of the Italian Renaissance came a rebirth in the design and planting of elaborate gardens including elements such as water in pools, fountains, and cascades, as well as the display of sculpture and sundials. Formal gardens became a popular art form and symmetrical gardens with neatly cropped hedges were cultivated everywhere.

Two centuries later formal garden cultivation exploded to magnificent proportions during the reign of Louis XIV of France. French Renaissance gardens covered vast areas with foliage arranged in symmetrical designs. Huge gardens and parks, including the famous gardens of Versailles, were designed by the master of the formal gardens, landscape architect André Le Notre.

Westward, in England, formal designs grew increasingly popular. The English, living in smaller Elizabethan homes, scaled down the formal garden and added fragrant herbs and flowers. Later, English settlers brought the art to colonial America. Today, Williamsburg, Virginia, contains the best examples of authentic eighteenth-century formal gardens in this country.

By the beginning of the twentieth century when eclectic styles had replaced the colonial, federal and Victorian, the formal garden gave way to the informal designs so common in the Florida landscape today. These newer styles more closely match the land, the homes, the neighborhoods, and the free-flowing lifestyles of today's home-dwellers.

The formal gardens of yesteryear are rare in the Florida landscape and are often confined to historical attractions such as Miami's Villa Vizcaya where visitors can enjoy viewing ten acres of Italian Renaissance-inspired formal gardens of a quality unmatched in the Western world.

Today, there are plenty of opportunities for Florida homeowners and landscape designers to explore and revive the creation and enjoyment of formal gardens.

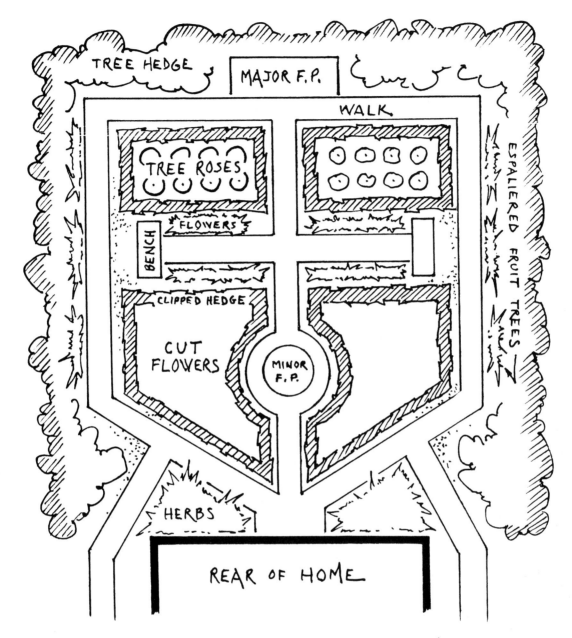

SMALL FORMAL GARDEN

This illustration shows the typical elements of a formal garden:

1. Placement of the garden in the rear yard.
2. Complete tree-hedge enclosure to isolate the garden from the surrounding neighborhood.
3. A major axis down the center of the garden terminating in a major focal point such as an arbor-covered seat, fountain, or statue.
4. Minor axes leading to benches or bird baths.
5. Mirror-image symmetry.
6. Geometric walks framed in close-clipped, low hedges such as yaupon holly, *Severinia buxifolia*, ixora, orange jasmine, or podocarpus.
7. Geometric beds of tree roses.
8. Minor focal point of a sundial or a sculpture placed closer to the home.
9. Espaliered fruit trees framing the garden.
10. Beds of annuals, perennials, and flowering bulbs for seasonal change.
11. Patches of herbs, culinary and medicinal.
12. Remaining bare ground filled in with ground cover such as liriope, mondograss, spider plants, or ivy.
13. Entire grassless, formal garden is designed to be visually enjoyed from the house as well as from anyplace in the garden.

PROMISE A ROSE GARDEN—Especially one in a formal setting. Our national flower is here cultivated amid formal paths, closely cropped hedges, and a tall, rustic privacy fence.

A FORMAL GARDEN—Reminiscent of old Williamsburg this carefully cropped *Severinia buxifolia* jogs around a bed of newly planted calendulas that will soon burst into brilliant orange. The hedge walls taper to allow sun to play upon the lower leaves. Symmetrical balance is readily apparent in this formal garden.

Museum of Fine Arts, St. Petersburg

Judge your landscape for beauty

Once again walk over the area you plan to landscape, holding your plans in your hand. Note where all plantings, beds, and constructions will be. Evaluate the appearance of the proposed landscape with respect to the principles of aesthetic design. All problems, whether related to a breach of beauty or function, should be discovered and solved in the planning stage before the dollar investment is made.

The following list of considerations will help you make your evaluation.

A. VIEWS FROM THE HOUSE

1. From the house and patio area (private area), are the lawn and surroundings free from unsightly views such as trash cans, tools, compost pile, clothesline, poorly developed neighboring lots, smokestacks in the distance?
2. Does the landscape take advantage of good views in the immediate area (such as a golf course, lake, or woods)?

B. VIEWS OF THE HOUSE

1. Is the house properly framed by trees above and beyond the roof line, with appropriate corner and foundation plantings to break up harsh architectural lines? Does the eye rest on the entrance as the main focal point?
2. Are the vertical or horizontal lines of the home broken or enhanced by proper planting to make the house look taller or wider?

C. PLANT MATERIALS

1. Are the plants properly chosen to provide suitable proportion and scale between the lot and the house size?
2. Do plants appear crowded, overused, or too sparse?
3. Do plants provide year-round interest (color of flowers and foliage, unusual forms or bark)?
4. Are an appropriate number of accent plants used to create contrast?
5. Is there balance between specimen and fill plants; deciduous and evergreen; foliage and flower interest; needleleaf and broadleaf; large, medium, and small plants; rough textures and smooth?

D. CONSTRUCTION MATERIALS

1. Do decks, walks, walls, fences, ponds, pools, or sheds exist which are tied to the house through similar materials, textures, or color?
2. Are tables, benches, chairs (portable or moveable) appropriately placed?
3. Is there any garden art, such as sculpture, a sundial, a birdbath or a fountain, etc., being used as a focal point? How effective is the placement?
4. How effective are the other construction items used, such as containers for plants, a wishing well, a foot bridge, a barbecue or the lathing, bricks or small stones used for surfacing?

E. DESIGN

1. Does the juncture of the lawn area and the border provide a sense of flow and rhythm through the use of strong, sweeping lines?
2. Is the landscape balanced either symmetrically or asymmetrically?
3. Are there common textures and repetitions among the parts to provide unity throughout the landscape?
4. Is simplicity maintained through axis lines and focalization?
5. In small landscapes is there an illusion of depth?

F. UNIQUE IDEAS

1. Are the other senses besides sight appealed to via running or trickling water or wind chimes (hearing), fragrant odors (smell), edible fruits or berries (taste), velvety foliage or appealingly textured objects (touch)?
2. Is the landscape equipped with lights to silhouette trunks and limbs of trees, to provide evening recreation, to light a path, to show off night-blooming plants, or to reflect shadows on a wall or patio floor?
3. Does the landscape include a pool, furniture, animals, outdoor cooking facilities, music?
4. Are there any unique construction features such as a sheltered patio bar or an unusual fence design?
5. If the landscape has a theme (Japanese, Polynesian, formal, or other), are the features of the theme consistent? Do they promote unity in the landscape?

H A P T E R

Three

FOUR SPLASH WATERFALL—Carefully balanced boulders are locked into place by concrete (wedged in their backsides out of sight). Note the pleasing sweep of the eye created by the play of plant heights circling the main focal point—the splashing water. The framing plants, starting left, then clockwise, are the hardy, giant bird of paradise (*Strelitzia nicolai*), *Nandina domestica*, *Dracaena marginata*, and the low *Carissa* 'Boxwood Beauty.'

Construction in your landscape

Construction features are those *non-living* things deliberately placed in a landscape. Almost every landscape will benefit from their presence. They may be things of beauty such as boulders, driftwood or sculpture. Or they may be functional pieces for use as benches or barbeques. Some may be necessities—a gate, lighting for a garden path, or play equipment. Others may be placed purely for enrichment—a waterfall, a swimming pool or a fireplace.

The construction features that you select and place, more than anything else, determine how much a landscape will be used and enjoyed. There must be convenience, comfort, and recreation in home landscapes in order to entice homeowners to leave their homes and enter their yards.

There are many considerations involved. Will there be sufficient solid-surface walks and patios? Will there be a patio roof or a lattice to provide a sheltered feeling? Will furniture be comfortable to sit on? Would decks afford pleasing views and vistas not seen from the house? Would the area be enhanced by a quaint little footbridge to cross or a gazebo to discover?

Besides making the landscape usable, construction features are aesthetically transitional. They help to tie the landscape to the house. A good starting point is to examine the type of wood, concrete, or stone used in the home and duplicate these materials in your construction ideas. Match the color of garden benches to the trim on the house. Face a barbeque with the same flagstone facing as on the house. Design the mailbox to repeat the lines of the home.

And finally, make sure your construction items will further the development of UBS. The concept of *unity* tells us that a rugged, rough-sawn patio roof will match the rough-sawn timbers accenting the home's basic architecture. *Balance* suggests that the construction features be in scale with the house and that they be in proportion to the entire landscape. *Simplicity* says to avoid using too many construction items. Don't make the landscape so busy with objects that the overall aesthetic appeal is lost.

The following construction features designed by others may generate some ideas for your landscape.

Build a brick walkway

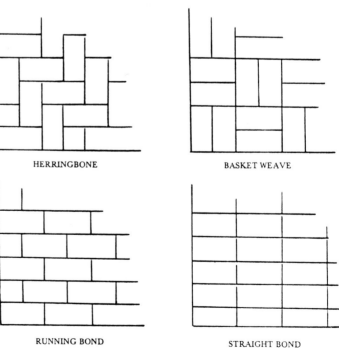

FILL SAND

SUBSOIL

To mark dimensions, pour flour or lime on the lawn where the new walkway will be. Remove the sod, two to three inches deep, and tamp the subsoil firm. Dig the edges deep enough to stand a row of bricks on end, to frame and support the walkway. A 1″ x 4″ cut the exact width of the walkway will help to keep its edges parallel. Inside the brick frame add two inches of sand and wet it for compaction. Then, lay bricks horizontally on the sand. When the walkway is finished, sweep a dry mixture of 50:50 sand and cement into the cracks between the bricks. Then, soak it thoroughly with water to set the concrete. Excess concrete left to dry on the surface will create an antique effect from inexpensive, plain brick.

Design brick patterns for patio & walks

Herringbone and basketweave are reminiscent of colonial times and work well with homes that match this architecture. More modern homes would use running bond or straight bond. Experiment with other patterns with a pencil and paper before you begin construction.

HERRINGBONE

BASKET WEAVE

RUNNING BOND

STRAIGHT BOND

Construct your own walkway

Cut paper patterns in various shapes and lay them on the lawn. With a trowel or machete cut around these pattern shapes and remove the sod (two to three inches deep). Pour ready-mix concrete into the holes. For an interesting texture set small chunks of ice into the con-crete surface before it hardens. This trick will produce an interesting, non-slip, Swiss cheese surface. Walkways of this type work well in all grasses except the creeping va-rieties (such as St. Augustine) that require constant maintenance to keep runners off the concrete.

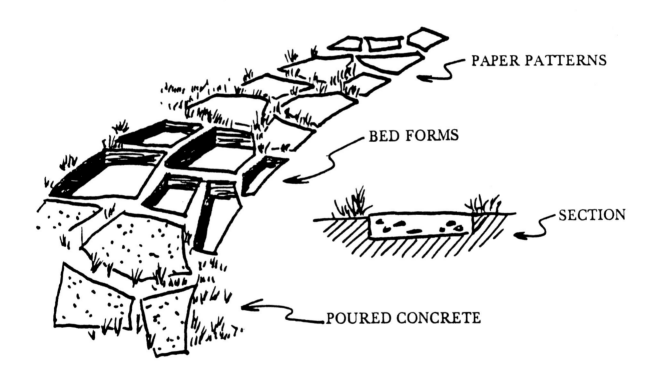

PAPER PATTERNS

BED FORMS

SECTION

POURED CONCRETE

Design driveways

If not designed properly, driveways present a real problem in the landscape. Whenever possible plan to provide enough off-street parking for all vehicles and off-street turnaround space to avoid having to back cars out onto busy thoroughfares. The following dimensions will allow sufficient turn and park space for full-size vehicles and vans. Single drives should be 8 to 10 feet wide, while doubles should be 16 feet wide.

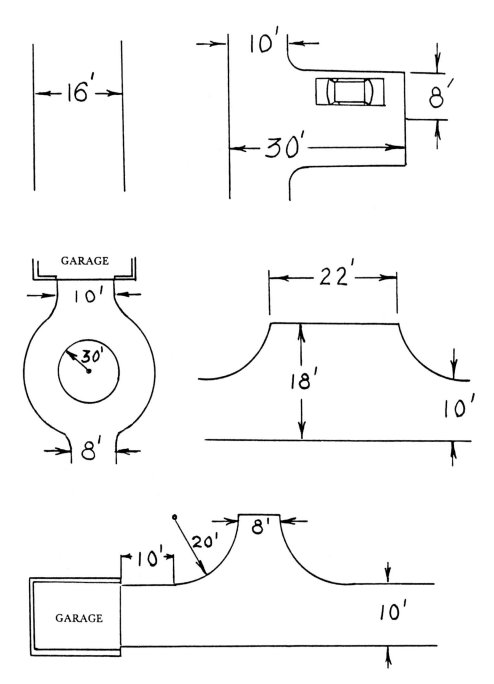

Build a reflection pool

Dig a freeform pool in front of a tall tree (or shrub mass) to catch its reflection on the pool's surface. For easy maintenance, avoid plants that drop leaves. Pour six inches of concrete and top with a sealer. Build in a couple of planting ledges for plants that grow in shallow water.

Edge the pool with rocks or patio stones for a natural effect. Add aquatic plants, especially water lilies, which should be kept in plant tubs of rich soil. Add lights, goldfish, and a small recirculating fountain for the final touch. (Fish will eat mosquito larvae.)

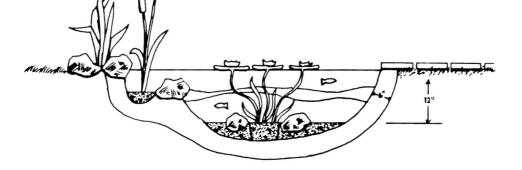

Make a mini storage area

Construct an attractive 4½-foot-high fence using 4' x 8' sheets of marine plywood kept rigid by 2" x 2"s and framed in 2" x 4"s. Support posts are made of pressure-treated 4" x 4"s, set two feet into the ground. The floor is river gravel laid over a sheet of black plastic (to keep out weeds). When finished, the storage area measures 16 feet square, plenty of room for odds-and-ends storage. Enclosure can be left natural or stained or painted to match the house.

Design a reflection pool

Reflection pools take many shapes and sizes. Some reflect cloud-filled skies. But the best ones are placed near a cluster of palms or other trees, or beside a boulder outcropping. This small home lot features the pool, in front of a palm and surrounded by a solid-surface deck and low-maintenance plantings.

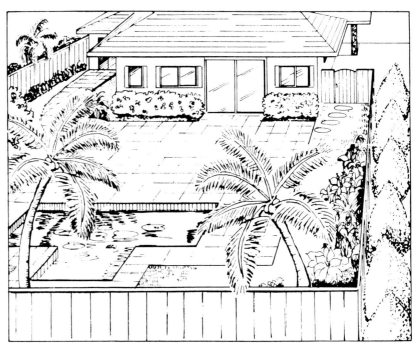

Landscape for outdoor living

An outdoor living room will receive lots of use because of its well-planned construction features. It provides: a floor with a solid surface, a privacy enclosure, a sheltered feeling (from the tall palms) and comfort elements usually found indoors—a bench and chairs, wall decorations, cooking facilities and lights.

HOUSE ON A HILL—Laced with the delicacy of soft, white petunias this blockade planter keeps the landscape from plunging into the street. Notice the timbers are four high on the street side, one high farther up the lawn's incline. The permanent plantings are 'San José' junipers and standard princess flower trees (*Tibouchina semidecandra*).

SPLIT RAIL FENCING—Cypress is a readily available timber in Florida and is used to make outdoor structures, especially fences in many patterns: basketweave, stockade, smooth rail, and rugged split rail. The zig-zag layout avoids the use of nails and adds a touch of early Americana. The background trees are specimens of the Florida state tree, the cabbage palm (*Sabal palmetto*). These palms were used by Florida's native Indians, who ate the cabbage heart, cut the palm fronds to cover their homes and start fires, and made boats from the trunks.

MINIMUM MAINTENANCE ENTRY—Large, poured concrete blocks are separated by no-mow artificial turf producing a uniquely patterned wide driveway that sweeps across the front of the home.

A SIX-SIDED IDEA—Whopping hexagonal stepping-stones laid geometrically form a striking, sturdy surface entry. Framing foliage encircles the setting and attracts your eye to the entry cove. Notice blooming pampas grass to the left.

Design: Robert Neal, ASLA

THE LAYERED LOOK—Vertical railroad ties placed in a sloping terrain give a layered look to the landscape and support plantings at two levels. Note the Japanese lantern placed in an Oriental bed of gravel and larger, island rocks.

INTERESTING USE OF ROCKS—Limestone rocks permit the terrain to slope upward from the street for visual interest while leaving the tree safe and undisturbed at its original planted depth. The lawn stops short of the tree trunk to keep mowing maintenance to a minimum.

Design: Sunset Landscape Co., Naples

INVITING, YES?—An empty bench is an open invitation, especially when nestled in an attractive pocket featuring a brick deck and wooden steps for easy access.

BENCH MADE TO LAST—Thick cypress timbers bolted in place and attached to 4" x 4" pressure-treated pine posts guarantee this bench's maximum longevity. Pressure-treated pine provides the best resistance against the subterranean termites and wood rots of Florida soils—much better than redwood or cypress. The framing shrubs are hibiscus.

THE WALKWAY THAT WINDS—Here traffic flow is enhanced by common bricks set upon two inches of sand. Vertical bricks buried along the edge hold the walkway in place as it winds through this lush bed of springeri fern (*Asparagus sprengeri*) accented with a weeping bottlebrush tree (*Callistemon citrinus*).

HOUSE ON A LAKE—Creosote pilings set against a bank flow like ripples on a lake. The pilings also form the curving edge of a circular patio, the perfect spot for comfortable furniture and large pots of flowers.

BILLY GOATS GRUFF—Seemingly from fairy tale land, this man-sized footbridge surely must have a couple of trolls hiding under its raised floor. A structure of this scale works great in a park, playground, or on the spacious grounds of a sizable residence of similar construction.

A FAIRYLAND COVERUP—A quaint little wishing well full of profusely blooming geraniums stands at the head of an entry drive. Concealed in the well's rafters, almost unnoticeable, is an otherwise ugly metal mailbox.

BRICK AND BOARD TO HIDE A VIEW—Like a giant serpent stretched in the sun this meandering walkway of discarded road brick winds around plants. The same brick is used with rough-sawn cypress laid board-on-board to create a stately wall that blocks an undesirable vista. The young European fan palm (*Chamaerops humilis*) is hardy everywhere in the state.

Design: Robert Slatinsky, St. Petersburg

THE TIE THAT BINDS—Tall, vertical railroad ties with concrete step surfaces support a heavy sod bank. Even in a heavy rain-storm the strength of this wall is enormous. Its vertical ties are secured with several dead-man anchors.

Designed and installed by Dade County's Everglades Sod and Landscape, Inc.

LIFE AND DEATH OF A MAILBOX PLANTER—In the spring, brilliantly colored *Amaranthus* 'tricolor' enwrapped the mailbox at the author's home. That fall scarlet red petunias were planted to bloom through the winter. Early next summer found dancing, purple balls of globe amaranth. But by next fall, after hurricane Elena, the author's son said, "Pop, what happened to our flower bed?"

DITTO DESIGN—Like an assembly of street signs pointing straight up, the roof lines on the home are mimicked in this little mailbox house.

Design: Florian Hesse, St. Petersburg

COUNTRY CORNER—A provincial wooden mailbox, complete with wooden flag, rests comfortably at the end of a tiered planter box whose timbers are notched log cabin fashion. This rural island is topped off with colorful flowers and a small holly (*Ilex opaca* 'East Palatka') just loaded with bright red berries.

AVIARY HOTEL—Bird lovers love a bird house of this scale (and so do the birds). The structure is made of pressure-treated pine, stained to match the cedar shakes and welded, 2″ x 4″ mesh, galvanized fencing.

DOUBLE ROLE PATIO—Bricks set on an inch of sand are held in place with dry cement which was swept into the cracks, then wet down and dried. The patio serves as an aqueduct to carry hundreds of gallons of water off an oversized driveway during the rainy season. The free-style planter displays a healthy *Ligustrum lucidum* and colorful annuals planted twice a year. Annuals twice a year? Yes. In Florida, we are blessed with two flower seasons a year, spring and fall.

Design: Mac Perry, St. Petersburg

WRAPAROUND DECK—This versatile deck overlooking the patio connects entrances at three different points and provides useful sheltered areas below. The columnar evergreens are Italian Cypress (*Cupressus sempervirens*). A large-leaf *Philodendron sellome* wraps around the deck corner.

TEXTURES GALORE—The wall is traditional brick while the concrete and tile on the floor are a more contemporary combination. Both elements are pulled together by a couple of tubs holding flowers which gently spill over their sides.

CAMOUFLAGED CONTAINER—Trash cans are always needed in the landscape, but they can be unsightly. This one is tastefully concealed in a redwood frame. A small latch-lock secures the wide-swinging access door.

A HANDSOME HIDEOUT—Here at the edge of the jungle is a low, rough-sawn fence angled to direct cars into the driveway. Who would know its real purpose is to hide garbage cans?

REDUCING MUD PUDDLES—Every entry door needs a solid surface to eliminate wear on the lawn. Here chunks of railroad ties do the job.

RECTANGLESCAPING—Treatments using landscape rounds are endless. Here their vertical and horizontal lines echo the linearity of the sidewalk and the planking of the wall, creating unity.

MOUND EXAGGERATED—Emphasize a raised plant bed by installing pressure-treated rounds of varying lengths that will seem to taper to the ground. Each round should be set at least eight inches deep.

ELEGANT PATIO—Delicate north Florida dogwood blossoms (*Cornus florida*) enhance this liriope laced patio in Brooksville. The shrub at the corner of the patio is *Magnolia fuscata*.

Rogers Christmas House, Brooksville

STURDY FOOTBRIDGE—Stable structures like this built of pressure-treated pine, if set on sawed-off, used telephone poles, can span creek beds for many years.

A WALL NATURALLY—Like the Great Wall of China, stones were carefully placed to separate the inner garden from the bay at this seaside residence.

THE LAWN THAT ISN'T—For a low-maintenance surface this Pass-a-Grille homeowner uses Chattahoochee river gravel. Emerging weeds are quickly snuffed with a trigger sprayer containing a contact herbicide.

Design: Joan Haley, Pass-a-Grille

ROAD BRICK—Used brick makes a charmingly rustic patio floor which doesn't require perfection in its concrete work.
Design: Smith Nursery, Largo

WOODEN RETAINING WALL—More natural than concrete, railroad ties, stacked five high and back supported, retain a bed of shrubs and a focal planting of spineless yucca (*Yucca elephantipes*). Notice how the newly planted *Cocos plumosa* palms are "boarded" together for support.

TRANSITIONAL PRIVACY FENCE—This tongue-and-groove privacy fence is tied to the house literally and aesthetically. The texture of its rectangular, rough-sawn beams is echoed at ground level by sawed-off railroad ties. Low, medium, and tall plantings are 'San José' juniper, *Ligustrum lucidum* 'Howardi' (with bright yellow leaves), and a bottlebrush tree (*Callistemon citrinus*).

SPRINGTIME QUAINTNESS—Nestled under the arms of a hardy oak this Gainesville Cape Cod home is made quaint by a curving brick walkway and simple plantings enclosed by a small, white picket fence.

WINTER PROTECTION—Corrugated fiberglass softly diffuses the light without reducing its foot-candle power. Tall pines (or shade cloth) will reduce light intensity. Protection of an orchid collection from too much direct light and winter cold is the purpose of this north Florida greenhouse.

GABLED PUMP HOUSE—Hidden in an obscure pocket of the landscape is a pump house (literally) complete with gables. Use CDX or marine plywood in construction for longer life. The structure not only hides the sprinkler system pump but also reduces its noise.

CONTINUING A GOOD THING—Duplicate beds of 'Evergreen Giant' liriope and live oaks give the impression that the walkway cuts through a single bed. This design technique allows viewers to participate in the landscape. As they pass through they become part of the planting bed.

BOARDWALK BEAUTY—A walkway of pressure-treated 2" x 6"s reduces turf wear in an already low corner. The walkway passes between a *Philodendron sellome* and a pair of colorful shrubs, a copper plant (*Acalypha wilkesiana*) and a croton (*Codiaeum variegatum*) that will soon grow large enough to hide the air conditioner.

Residence: Sam and Bonnie Bottoms

NATURALIZED POOL—Rocklike decking and a huge boulder waterfall give this handsome West Palm Beach pool the old swimming hole appeal. Note the fountain hurling streams of water into the pool for textural and auditory excitement.

Design: Robert L. Neal, ASLA
Photo: L. L. Finton

C H A P T E R *four*

Color
in your
landscape

Nothing moves the emotions of the gardener more than a fresh splash of color in the landscape. Whether it is a vibrant mass of dew-glistened globe amaranth dancing in the freshness of early morning or the splatter of white dogwood bracts set against a wooded darkness heralding the long-awaited spring, each of us is drawn to stop and stare and to remember.

Take a moment and walk with me through my spring color garden at the front of my house and see what I mean.

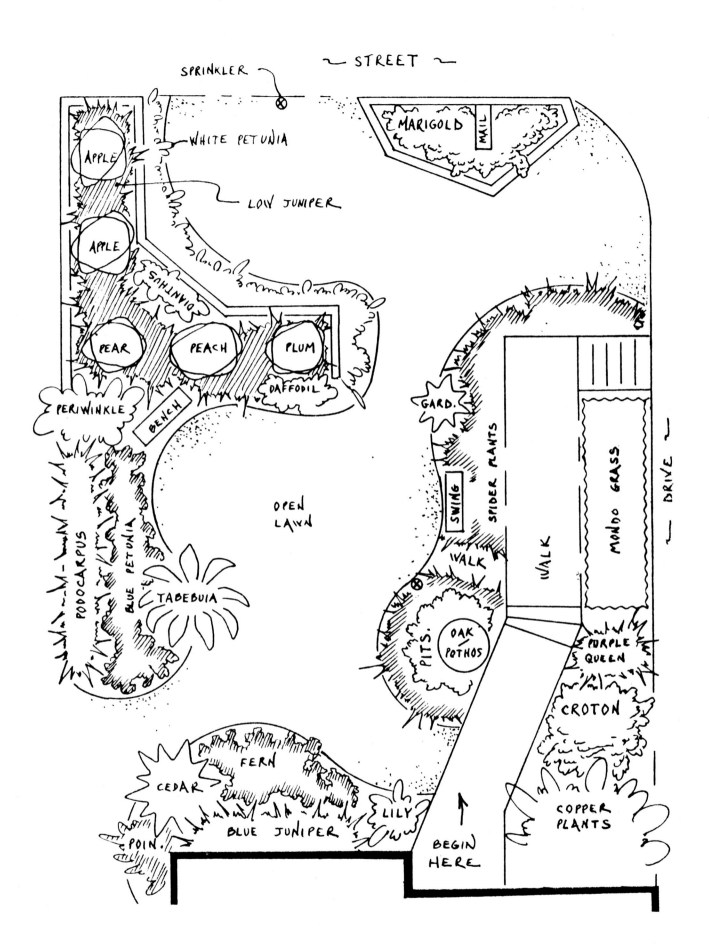

My Color Garden

As we step from the front door, notice that we are much higher than the street and my neighbors. My home sits atop a mound built thousands of years ago by native American mound builders, perhaps the aggressive Calusa Indians who dwelled along the shore of Boca Ceiga Bay and southward. The thought is intriguing that below us, discarded upon this early kitchen midden, are artifacts such as broken pottery and animal bones. The mound beautifully displays my garden from the street view. But there is a problem with the mound. Ninety-nine percent of it is discarded oyster, clam, and scallop shells collected and discarded by its Indian builders. That gave me trouble at first because plant beds had to be dug out with a pick and shovel and amended with peat, manure, and top soil to provide a good soil base.

As we proceed along the walkway on the right is a color bed of crotons. These are the most colorfully leaved plants in the world with their vibrant shades of yellow, orange, red, green, and white. I plant them closest to the entry door. Behind them is a huge copper plant with rich red foliage that matches the brick walls of my home. In front, purple queen creeps along as a ground cover showing off its violet hue. Because they each have a shade of red in them, the violet and red and brick are color cousins and go well together. Filling in the rest of the bed is a carefree mass of mondo grass.

Let's turn left now and enter the color garden. Don't step on those Easter lilies. They are about bloomed out. (I should have staked them for better display. I'll put that on my list of gardening chores.)

Farther along is this wall planting. Next to the house are blue vase junipers, evergreens with a blue tint. And in front of them springeri fern, an evergreen with a yellow tint. That makes them color cousins too. They have green in common. At the corner of the house a red cedar is a neutral green, and its needlelike leaves match the

plants in the rest of the bed. This is a permanent bed with no yearly variation. Its perennial nature adds a subtle color accent to the landscape.

We keep the cedar trimmed like a Christmas tree because the kids like to hang lights on it in December. Behind the cedar is a large poinsettia. You can't see it now because it has been pruned. But by Christmas its bright red bracts will be spilling around the cedar and it will be nearly ten feet tall. Poinsettia will flourish if it is pruned properly.

Now turn around and look at this giant live oak. Its twisting arms stretch over most of the yard and keep the hot summer sun from burning the flowers. That large-leaf vine covering the trunk is pothos. Some of those leaves are two feet long. On freezing nights we have to hang a blanket around them for protection.

See how your eye starts at the pothos, ten feet up, sweeps down across the surrounding pittosporum to the spider plant ground cover at its base. (I call this progression the football-stadium effect. The plants are the spectators in the grandstand and we are the players looking up at them.)

The white in the spider plants matches the variegation in the pothos but the two are kept separated by the deep, shiny green of the pittosporum. See how these color cousins work together. The spider plants start at the front door, surround the pittosporum, dip behind our front yard swing, wrap the grafted gardenia tree and spill the rest of the way down the hill, locking the entire bed into a unified whole.

Look at the size of those gardenia buds. Already I can smell the fragrance of those gorgeous white flowers. They'll burst into bloom in about two more weeks.

By the way, this soft turf is Floratam St. Augustine. It resists most pest problems. I thoroughly water it and all the other plants twice a week with just two pop-up sprinklers. Keeping it dry the rest of the week helps resist weeds and fungus. It does well in this filtered sunlight. The shell mound doesn't seem to bother it. See how it directs traffic through the landscape? And there's not one plant growing in the sod. I can mow it in ten minutes.

Along the left border is my largest bed. The border hedge is a six-foot row of weeping podocarpus. It provides partial enclosure during the day and at night keeps auto lights out of my eyes where I sit here under these moonlit boughs.

At its base. is a mass of richly colored 'Ultra Blue' petunias. I like petunias because they come in so many colors, are really easy to grow, and will bloom here in central Florida from September till late spring when the heat burns them out. Both the 'grandiflora' and the newer 'multiflora' types are excellent choices, but they must be planted as a cool-season flower. They'll even survive a light freeze.

At the front of this bed is my favorite small tree, *Tabebuia argentea*. The yellow blooms are splendid in the spring and complement the blue petunias.

Moving right along you see my garden bench and behind it a giant display of pink periwinkle planted by a friendly bird who dropped a seed at the edge of the planter. That plant alone has over one thousand blooms. (Talk about easy to grow.)

Here on the point is a pocket of daffodils. They don't normally grow in Florida, so I had to refrigerate the bulbs before planting. I like those yellow trumpet flowers because they remind me of my youth in Virginia. As do those five fruit trees lining the raised bed. I once had five beautiful, purple flowering Tibochina trees there but a freeze got them. The fruit trees are Florida varieties but withstand cold and provide spring blossoms. I like them better.

Massed beneath the fruit trees and covering much of this railroad tie bed are 'San José' junipers. They never get taller than a foot and provide a permanence

to the bed when I have to replant the annuals.

Also, I have more pockets of annuals here where there is more sunlight. These flowers like at least six hours of sun a day. At the top of the raised railroad tie bed are dianthus. Their red color is set off by bold white 'Glacier' petunias that border the bottom of the railroad tie. White is the strongest color in the landscape and can be seen from two blocks away while reds and blues tend to fade into the landscape.

My largest mass of flowers is there around the mailbox. That bed is sterilized with Vapam and replanted every six months. Sterilization is important to reduce the ever-returning nematode population that often contaminates plant beds in our warm Florida soils. (Don't sterilize beds containing permanent plants.) I've just removed a delicate mass of purple globe amaranth that danced its hundreds of blooms all winter. The new plants are 'Jubilee' marigolds. Marigolds, (especially the triploid hybrids, a cross between the compact French and the large-flowered American), constitute the longest, boldest and most trouble-free summer annual in the landscape. They come in yellow, orange, red, and, now, white.

Well, that's my spring color garden. I put most of my flowers in pockets or beds in the front landscape because that's where they can be enjoyed by a larger number of people. And the real beauty is that if you return in six months the garden will be different—with new colors, new fragrances. It is an ever-changing pleasure garden that gives me hours of joy with only minutes of attention each week, year-round.

When planning your color garden, design pockets of color-splash annuals in separate beds and amongst the permanent beds. To help you select, here is a chart I find helpful. It is provided by the Florida Cooperative Extension Service.

PLANTING GUIDE FOR ANNUALS

Name	Exposure			Cold Tolerance	North Florida		Central Florida		South Florida		Spacing (inches)
	Full Sun	Sun—A.M. or P.M.	No Direct Sun		Planting Date	Removal Date	Planting Date	Removal Date	Planting Date	Removal Date	
Ageratum	XX			Tender	Mar. 1-15	Aug.	Feb. 15-Mar. 15	July	Feb. 1-Mar. 1	June	10-12
Alyssum	XX			Tender	Mar. 1-15	July	Feb. 15-Mar. 15	July	Oct. 1-15 Feb. 1-Mar. 1	Mar. June	6
Amaranthus	XX			Tender	Mar. 15-30	Sept.	Mar. 15-30	July	July-Aug. Mar. 1-15	First Frost July	14-18
Asters	XX			Tender	Mar. 1-15	July	Feb. 15-28	June	Oct.-Feb.	June	12
Baby's Breath	XX	X		Hardy	Feb. 15-Mar. 15	June	Feb.-Mar.	June	Aug.-Dec.	Mar.-Apr.	12
Balsam	XX	X		Tender	Mar. 15-30	Aug.	Mar. 1-30	July	Mar. 1-30	June-July	8-12
Begonia (Nonstop)		XX	X	Tender	Mar. 1-15	June	Feb. 15-28	May	Nov.-Mar.	May	12-14
Begonia (Tuberous)		X	XX	Tender	Mar. 1-15	June	Feb. 15-28	May	Oct.-Jan.	Apr.	12-14
Begonia (Wax)	XX	X		Tender	Mar. 15-30	Sept.-Oct.	Feb. 15-28	Sept.	Sept.-Nov.	Aug.	12-14
Browallia	XX	X		Hardy	Mar. 1-15	Aug.	Feb. 15-28	Aug.	Oct.-Feb.	Aug.	12
Calendula	XX			Hardy	Feb.-Mar.	June	Nov.-Feb.	June	Jan.-Mar.	May	8-10
Carnation (China Doll)	XX			Hardy	Nov.-Feb..28	June	Nov.-Feb. 28	May	Oct.-Jan. 15	Apr.	8-10
Celosia	XX			Tender	Mar. 15-July	Seed Set	Mar.-July	Seed Set	Feb.-Sept.	Seed Set	14
Coleus	X	XX		Tender	Apr.-Aug.	Oct.	Apr.-Aug.	Oct.-Nov.	Mar.-Sept.	First Frost	18-24
Calliopsis	XX	X		Hardy	Mar.-May	First Frost	Mar.-May	First Frost	Feb.-June	First Frost	12
Cosmos	XX			Tender	Mar. 15	Aug.	Feb.	July	Nov.-Feb.	June	12-14
Crossandra		XX	XX	Tender	May-July	Oct.	Apr.-July	Oct.	Mar.-Aug.	Nov.	8-12
Dahlia	X	XX		Tender	Mar. 15-30	Aug.	Mar. 1-15	Aug.	Sept.-Dec.	July	18-20
Dianthus	XX			Hardy	Feb.	July-Aug.	Feb.	July	Oct.-Feb.	June	10-12
Digitalis (Fox glove)	XX	X		Hardy	Sept.-Dec.	July	Sept.-Dec.	July	Not recommended		12
Dusty Miller	XX	X		Tender	Feb.-Apr.	Sept.	Feb.-Apr.	Aug.	Oct.-Mar.	Aug.	12
Exacum	XX	XX		Tender	Mar.-July	When overgrown	Mar.-July	When overgrown	Feb.-Oct.	When overgrown	12
Gaillardia	XX	X		Semi-Hardy	Mar.-May	Aug.	Mar.-May	Aug.	Feb.-May	Aug.	12-18
Gazania	XX			Tender	Mar.-May	Nov.	Feb. 15-May	Nov.	Nov.-May	Nov.	8
Geranium	XX	X		Tender	Mar.-Apr.	July	Feb.-Mar.	July	Oct.-Mar.	June	16-30
Hollyhock (Althaea rosea)	XX	X		Hardy	Mar. 15-June	First Frost	Feb. 15-July	First Frost	Aug.-Sept.	First Frost	12

Name	Exposure			Cold Tolerance	North Florida		Central Florida		South Florida		Spacing (inches)
	Full Sun	Sun—A.M. or P.M.	No Direct Sun		Planting Date	Removal Date	Planting Date	Removal Date	Planting Date	Removal Date	
Impatiens		XX	X	Tender	Mar. 15-July	First Frost	Mar. 1-July	First Frost	Sept.-June	First Frost	8-12
Kalanchoe	XX	X		Tender	May-July	First Frost	May-Sept.	First Frost	Sept.-Dec.	First Frost	12
Lobelia	XX	X		Tender	Mar. 15-Apr.	Aug.	Feb. 15-Apr.	Aug.	Sept.-Feb.	July	6-8
Marguerite Daisy	XX			Tender	Feb. 15-Apr.	June-July	Feb.-Apr.	June-July	Oct.-Feb.	June	12-14
Marigold	XX			Tender	Mar. 15-May	3-4 months after planting	Mar.-Aug.	3-4 months after planting	Feb.-Dec.	3-4 months after planting	8-24
Nicotiana	XX	X		Tender	Mar. 15-July	Aug.-Sept.	Mar. 1-July	Aug.-Sept.	Feb.-May Aug.-Sept.	July-Aug. Apr.-May	16-24
Ornamental Pepper	XX			Tender	Mar.-July	Oct.	Mar.-July	Oct.	Mar.-Aug.	Nov.	8-10
Pansy	XX			Hardy	Oct.-Feb.	June	Oct.-Feb.	May	Oct.-Jan.	Apr.	10-14
Pentas	XX	X		Tender	Mar.-May	Leaf disease	Mar.-May	Leaf disease	All year	Leaf disease	12-14
Petunia	XX	X		Hardy	Oct.-Feb.	May-June	Oct.-Feb.	June	Sept.-Feb.	May	12-18
Phlox	XX			Hardy	Mar.-Apr.	Aug.	Mar.-Apr.	Aug.	Feb.-Mar.	July	8-14
Portulaca (Rose moss)	XX			Tender	Apr.-July	First Frost	Apr.-July	First Frost	Mar.-Aug.	First Frost	10-12
Rudbeckia	XX			Hardy	Mar.-Apr.	Aug.	Mar.-Apr.	Aug.	Feb.-Mar.	July	15-18
Salvia	XX	X		Tender	Mar. 15-Aug.	When deteriorated	Mar. 1-Aug.	When deteriorated	Feb. 15-Dec.	When deteriorated	8-12
Shasta Daisy	XX	X		Hardy	Oct.-Dec.	July	Oct.-Dec.	July	Not recommended		12
Snapdragon	XX	X		Hardy	Oct.-Feb.	June	Oct.-Feb.	May	Nov.-Feb.	Apr.-May	10-15
Statice	XX			Hardy	Feb. 15	June	Dec.-Jan.	June	Sept.-Jan.	May	8-10
Strawflower	XX			Tender	Mar. 15	Aug.	Feb.	July	Nov.-Feb.	June	12-14
Streptocarpus		XX	X	Tender	Mar.-Apr.	June	Mar.-Apr.	June	Feb.-Mar.	May	10
Sweet Williams	XX	X		Hardy	Mar.-Apr.	Aug.	Mar.-Apr.	Aug.	Feb.-Mar.	May	10-12
Thunbergia (alata)	XX	X		Tender	Mar.-May	First Frost	Mar.-May	First Frost	Feb.-Apr.	First Frost	8-10
Torenia	XX	X		Tender	Mar. 15-June	Leaf yellowing	Mar. 1-June	Leaf yellowing	Feb.-Oct.	Leaf yellowing	12-18
Verbena	XX			Hardy	Mar. 1-May	When undesired	Feb. 15-May	When undesired	Feb.-Apr. Sept.-Nov.	When undesired	12
Vinca (Catharanthus) (periwinkle)	XX	X		Tender	Mar.-July	When undesired	Feb. 15-July	When undesired	All year	When undesired	12
Zinnia	XX			Tender	Mar.-June	Leaf disease	Mar.-June	Leaf disease	Feb.-Mar. Aug.-Sept.	Leaf disease	12-15

Color cousins and complements

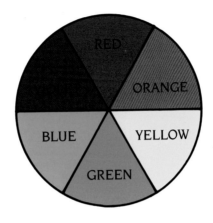

PRIMARY COLORS

RED
YELLOW
BLUE

SECONDARY COLORS

ORANGE
GREEN
VIOLET

In general, almost any colorful plant will improve a landscape, but an understanding of color cousins and complements will help you decide which colors work well together. It all begins with the color wheel—the same one used by artists in developing their pallets.

The three primary colors—red, yellow, and blue—are pure colors that cannot be made by mixing any combination of colors. However, when they are mixed they produce all the other colors. Each secondary color is made by mixing its two neighbors on the color wheel. For instance, to produce orange, simply mix red and yellow. As a matter of fact, if you planted a mixture of red and yellow flowers in a large bed and viewed it from a block away it would appear orange. Your eyes would make the blend. Look at the orange flowers in this book under a magnifying glass and you will see the tiny red and yellow dots that the printer uses to make orange.

By mixing primary colors in varying proportions and adding quantities of white and black, hundreds of tints, shades and tones are produced.

Color cousins are those adjacent colors on the color wheel that have one color in common. For instance, red, orange, and yellow are cousins because they are each related to orange. The yellow and red produce the orange. Likewise violet, blue, and green are cousins because each has blue in it. Color cousins are any two or three adjacent colors on the wheel. Commit this simple color wheel to memory because planting a bedful of color cousins is a good way to produce harmony. Color cousins always go well together. Red dianthus looks good with violet impatiens and orange gaillardia. If ninety percent of your bed is comprised of color cousins and ten percent is not related, an unpleasant result will occur.

On the other hand, the greatest contrast is produced when color complements are used. Complementary colors are opposites on the color wheel. Red is the complement of green, orange the complement of blue, and yellow the complement of violet. When a color is placed next to its complement both it and its complement appear more intense. To make a bed of yellow gloriosa daisies appear more brilliant, border them with a wide edging of violet ageratum. The key to planting complements is to use masses of both colors.

When selecting colors for your plant beds, besides thinking in terms of color cousins or color complements, also consider if flowers are for a summer bed (and can stand the heat) or if they must grow in the cooler winter months. Here are a few ideas for using cousins and complements in a flower bed.

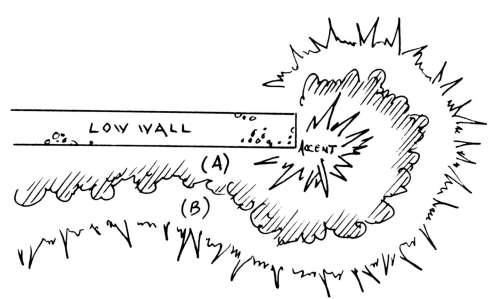

COLOR COUSINS FOR COOL MONTHS
Orange calendula (A) with red snapdragons (B)
Violet statice (A) with blue petunias (B)
Yellow digitalis (A) with orange nasturtium (B)

COLOR COUSINS FOR WARM MONTHS
Violet lisianthus (A) with red celosia (B)
Yellow cosmos (A) with orange marigolds (B)
Orange zinnia (A) with red and violet coleus (B)

COLOR COMPLEMENTS FOR COOL MONTHS
Violet asters (A) with yellow pansies (B)
Orange calendula (A) with blue ageratum (B)
White globe amaranth (A) with red geraniums (B)

COLOR COMPLEMENTS FOR WARM MONTHS
Blue dahlias (A) with orange zinnias (B)
Yellow gloriosa daisies (A) with violet impatiens (B)
Green kochia (A) with red salvia (B)

There is a wide assortment of white flowers including the silver dusty miller that can be used as a complement or cousin to any other color. White flowers are especially useful when they separate complementary colors or as border edging that defines a bed and segregates the flowers from the lawn. In this capacity whites serve as highlight or as a frame for the flower bed.

One unique quality about white flowers that is seldom recognized is that white is the most contrasting color in the landscape. Whites have a brilliance that is unparalleled by any other color. View a variety of flower colors from a block or two away and you will see that the whites are the only ones distinctly visible. (If I were to design an entry garden for a Florida tourist attraction and I wanted to catch the eye of all vehicles within eyesight of the entry, I would use great masses of whites layered up from six-inch alyssum through one-foot petunias, two-foot shasta daisies, and surrounded by a four- to eight-foot hedge of white oleanders, all set against a woodsy background of dark greens. The entry road and foot paths designed for closer viewing can pick up other colors, but beds seen from great distances seem to vibrate in whites.)

When choosing color plants for your garden there are many considerations to weigh—color cousins and complements, cool- or warm-month varieties, annuals or permanent shrubs and trees, short or tall varieties, low-maintenance or high-maintenance species, and susceptibility to insects, diseases, and nematodes.

Even color intensity becomes important. Photographers call the strength of a color, color saturation. Many years ago I viewed a huge bed of petunias at Longwood Gardens in Pennsylvania. The flowers were planted in blocks of very pale pinks, purples, and soft rose colors. I would never have selected any of those pale varieties alone but standing in the midst of all the delicate colors actually affected my emotions. I was transformed from a tired and weary tourist to a relaxed guest. The subtle colors softened my emotions and drew me into their subliminal world with tender caresses. A patch of intensely colored flowers anywhere in that garden would have ruined the whole effect, so consider color intensity when designing a color garden.

One additional consideration is warm colors versus cool colors. Warm yellows and reds go well together and show best in hot, summer gardens. The cooler blues, violets and greens go well together and should dominate the cool-season garden. When mixed together a complementary relationship is established.

Annuals are the fastest, cheapest, and most spectacular way to establish color in your garden. However, an abundance of flowering shrubs, trees, and ground covers are available to the Florida gardener that require less maintenance and show their colors at certain months of the year. To help you develop year-round color in your garden, Chapter Seven has a list of several flowering shrubs and trees showing their seasons of maximum color.

CHRYSANTHEMUMS with a wide variety of colors and shapes provide a delicate splash of color. Grown here in wooden barrel halves, if given uninterrupted darkness during fall nights, they will bloom each winter.

The luster of **BOUGAINVILLEA** in varying shades of red is one of the most colorful sights in the Florida landscape. Thorny vines can be forced into a shrub or allowed to sprawl over a tall trellis in full sunlight.

PERIWINKLE (*Catharanthus roseus*), called *Vinca rosea*, grown from seed to a two-foot ground cover, blooms profusely most of the year. Periwinkle prefers sandy soil and requires little maintenance.

FLAME VINE (*Pyrostegia ignea*) adds a startling spectacle to the late winter landscape in central and south Florida. Because the vine is a fast, rampant grower, allow it plenty of room to grow. Prune flame vine after its flowers fall.

CHENILLE PLANT (*Acalypha hispida*), also called red-hot cattail, grows to eight feet in warmer parts of the state. May lose its leaves in areas of cooler winters.

CROTON, the most colorful non-flowering shrub in the world, grows to ten feet in warmer areas of the state. These growing at Miami's Parrot Jungle display brilliant shades of reds, oranges, yellows, and deep purple.

PYRACANTHA COCCINEA (or **FIRETHORN**) can be used for espalier shaping and is capable of producing a great profusion of winter berries, either red or orange. Teague Perry, the author's four-year-old, proudly shows this off. Firethorn is not productive in south Florida.

CRAPE MYRTLE (*Lagerstromia indica*) blooms best in the summer and grows statewide. Its leaves usually fall in the winter. Its maximum height is only 20 feet.

GOLDENRAIN TREE (*Koelreuteria formosana*) is perhaps the most versatile shade tree. In winter it is bare. In spring, tiny, light green leaves emerge. In summer it blooms 18-inch masses of bright yellow flowers. And in fall the tree is covered with pink, papery capsules, as seen here. Goldenrain trees grow best in cooler portions of the state.

Here a handsome specimen basket of BURROW TAIL hangs in the morning sun over a bed of colorful annuals. Burrow tail needs protection from cold in north Florida.

CANNA with ornate flowers of red, white, yellow, buff, or pink blooms profusely during warm months. Canna should be planted in the full sun; its root stock should be divided every three years. It will die to the ground in cold locations and should be sprayed to reduce leaf caterpillars.

Spring brings out best in the north Florida landscape. Delicate pink flowers wrap around the still bare branches of the REDBUD tree (*Cercis canadensis*) to awaken the hibernating landscape. Redbuds grow to 30 feet.

Framing this home is the most popular flowering tree of north Florida, the flowering **DOGWOOD** (*Cornus florida*). Early each spring colorful bracts burst forth along the branches before the leaves appear. A red variety, 'Rubra,' is also available but doesn't do as well in Florida.

SPIREA THUNBERGII in north Florida displays a profusion of white flowers in late winter. The shrub prefers shifting shade and makes a good backdrop for darker shrubbery. S. *vanhouttei* is a similar, popular shrub often seen in the cooler regions.

TULIPS can be grown in Florida but new bulbs must be planted each spring. Purchase large bulbs in the fall and refrigerate them all winter. Add peat and 6-6-6 fertilizer to the planting bed. Plant five inches deep, eight inches apart, then stand back and wait for a magnificent display.

A blaze of color spreads below the delicate yellow of newly formed leaves at this commercial site. **AZALEAS** are available in whites, pinks, and various shades of red. They prefer a moist, acid soil and bloom from late winter to late spring.

The attention-getting **SHAVING BRUSH TREE** (*Pachira spp.*) is seen only in frost-free areas of south Florida where it grows to 30 feet. Flowers borne in late winter on bare branches have numerous red stamens that make up the brush. It's best to keep grass back from the roots.

ROYAL POINCIANA (*Delonix regia*), called **FLAMBOYANT** in the Caribbean, displays a huge umbrella of dazzling scarlet flowers each summer. This 40-foot specimen is tolerant of poor soils and mild salt drift and inspired the famous song of the trees—'Poinciana.

FIRECRACKER SHRUB is much more common in south Florida than in central Florida where it is killed back in cold winters. The shrub produces an explosion of delicate red flowers on slender branches that cascade over planter boxes. Plant firecracker shrubs where the cascade effect can be appreciated.

During the cool Christmas season, no flower excels the radiant **POINSETTIA** for maximum bloom. Prune 50% of the new growth in April, June, and August. Poinsettia comes in red, pink, and white and is killed to the ground by frost. Avoid planting near street lights because the plant needs darkness.

Here are four good ways to spruce up a border with vivid color.
Fibrous-rooted **BEGONIA** comes in red, white, and pink and blooms during winter months in central and south Florida.

IMPATIENS, also called **BALSAM,** are available in a number of colors. Plant in the spring. Impatiens are killed by frost.

Scarlet sage **SALVIA** displays lustrous red flowers on erect spikes. Plant salvia in front of darker shrubbery in the spring or summer.

CHICKEN GIZZARD (*Iresine herbstii*), pinched for low growth, displays rich, purple foliage in front of **FRENCH MARIGOLDS.** Both survive the hot Florida summers.

Massive, free-flowing beds of colorful annuals like these **PANSIES** are seen more commonly these days along Florida's highways and median strips. Flowers are replaced yearly, often with a different species for variety.

The dark, purplish foliage of **ALTERNANTHERA** used as a ground cover or border for taller plants turns to a brighter red to add sparkle to the winter landscape.

Height and color variation give this border its eye appeal. First there is the green lawn, then the silver **DUSTY MILLER**, followed by **FRENCH MARIGOLDS**, variegated *Ligustrum lucidum*, blue-tinted **BLUE VASE JUNIPER** and, finally, the dark green of **PODOCARPUS**.

A spectacular showing comes from the summer annual *AMARANTHUS TRICOLOR*. Space rear plants 18 inches apart. Space front plants 36 inches apart (and prune these to half height when they are two feet tall).

TABEBUIA ARGENTIA, an attractive, small tree, is common in Miami and Sarasota. Bold masses of yellow-gold flowers adorn its bare limbs in the early spring. The silver branches contort for added interest. The tree's maximum height is about 25 feet.

SNAPDRAGONS make a showy display. Plant them in full sun in the fall for winter bloom.

'Cockscomb' CELOSIA comes in red, yellow, orange, purple, and rose. The heavy, velvet flowers are always popular as an oddity. Dwarfs and taller varieties are available. Plant in the spring in full sun. To get a head start on the season, purchase young plants at garden centers.

Plant ZINNIAS in full sun in the spring for a riot of summer color. Also, spray them to avoid leaf spot fungus.

C H A P T E R *Five*

DANCE OF THE OAKS—Feathery textured native oaks dance before this double-doored entrance and provide a sheltered, protected effect without obstructing the view. An entry walkway comes in from the driveway (to the right) at this Clearwater home.

Hughes Homes

Ideas for entryways

The entrance to a home is the most important area in the landscape. It is here that all visitors will pass, here that you are likely to greet your guests, and from here that you will bid them safe journey when they depart.

The entrance, because of its location, must be a transitional area. It should have some elements of the home, such as a firm, spacious surface, a sense of enclosure, perhaps some furniture, and some elements of the outside such as shrubbery and potted plants.

The front door is the eye of the home. It is where a visitor looks to know more of the character of the home and its residents. The design of the door and the entryway should be given utmost attention. The plantings and construction features around the entryway are like eye shadow, mascara, and eye liner around the eyes. There can be too much or too little, unless you take care.

All the plantings around the entryway should be permanent and well manicured. Those of a dwarf variety requiring little pruning are recommended. Avoid using plants that drop their leaves in cooler months or plants with perennial pest problems. Likewise, avoid fast-growing, wild and bushy things or roses with thorns and months of poor appearance.

The farther the eye goes from the entryway toward the sides of the house, the larger and taller the plantings should be. This design technique creates a funnel effect that pulls the eye toward the entryway. Rarely should you ever block a view of the front door with any plant or construction feature. When this is done the home loses its warmth. Keep eye-level foliage to a minimum.

Another technique used to pull the eye toward the front door is to design the shape of the lawn or plant beds to point towards the door or to tilt tall palms in its direction.

Tubs of bold-colored flowers—geraniums, petunias, or marigolds—placed near the front door always say, "Welcome. This is a friendly place."

The most successful entryways have a "goodnight area." This is usually a small patio between the door and the driveway that is large enough for six or eight people, enclosed by a low wall or shrubbery, sheltered by a tree or large beams extending from the house, and perhaps even contains a bench or two. The area must have a firm, stable surface and should be lighted, preferably at the ground level, with mushroom lights. Here, hosts spend the last few moments with their guests, and this lasting impression of a cozy, friendly atmosphere will linger long after everyone has departed. In other words, the artistic design of your entryway can serve to project your feelings toward your guests.

And finally, an entryway must be functional. If there is room, provide as much off-street parking as is practical, offer vehicle turn-around space, keep grass minimized for lower maintenance, and avoid planting overpowering shrubs that will hide your home or block the view of oncoming cars when exiting from the driveway.

Look now at some entryways designed by professionals and see how they create attractive, functional environments that roll out the welcome mat.

Design a "goodnight area"

The "goodnight area" is where you bid fare-well to your guests. It is perhaps the most im-portant area of the landscape because it will be used by all visitors and provides the environ-ment for the final image your guests will retain. It should be close to the front door, spacious, hard surfaced, well lighted, and sheltered by over-hanging trees or a patio roof.

Fence your front yard

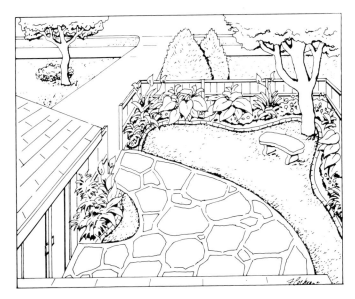

A three-foot fence provides privacy for you and an enclosure for your poodle, but does not block the view of the house. When designed in a free form and set back several feet from the front walkway there is ample opportunity to land-scape both sides of the fence with plenty of shrubs and trees. Notice the spacious, hard sur-faced goodnight area.

Landscape a circular drive

The island left by a circular drive should be landscaped with abundant shrubbery, boulders, sod, trees or palms, all chosen to match the other plants around the home. The area should be tied to the house, not to the street. A low fence can be added for privacy without blocking the view. This technique pulls the island into the overall landscape.

Create the funnel effect

To pull viewers' eyes to the main entryway (the eye of the home), plant larger trees at the outer edge of the landscape and at the corners of the home. Closer to the door, the shrubbery should be pruned shorter. Next to the door, plant low sprawling plants that display colorful flowers or variegated leaves. This technique funnels the entry for aesthetic balance. Additional framing is achieved by planting tall masses of trees in the rear yard to tower over the roof like a backdrop.

PRIVACY FRAMING—A tall but narrowly pruned and highly salt-tolerant sea grape hedge dresses a ten-foot wall offering beauty and privacy to the driveway entry of this seaside home.

"FOCALIZE" WITH ACCENT PLANTS—A superb focal point is created by a cluster of three Italian cypresses (*Cupressus sempervirens*) faced with a handsome, chest-high king sago palm (*Cycas revoluta*) placed against a bare wall. The wall locates the focus of the undulating gravel walkway leading to the front door.

Rutenberg Homes

SEMIPRIVATE ENTRANCE—While most entrances are highly visible, this double-doored version is located well away from sidewalk activity and street noise. This remoteness provides the landscaper with an opportunity to design a sweeping walkway that winds through an appealing thicket of shrubbery. Notice the backdrop effect provided by native trees for the roof line of this captivating home.

Hughes Homes

SPANISH ELEGANCE—Picturesque gumbo-limbo trees (*Bursera simaruba*) line the spacious, circular entry of this Palm Beach residence and provide semiprivacy.

FUNNEL EFFECT—Tall trees at the corner of the house, joined by medium trees closer to the door and low plantings near the door, funnel attention toward the front door. Funnel plantings are best tied together in a sweeping bed.

ANGLED WALK—A bed of ever-blooming 'Duc de rohan' azaleas is held back by an interesting railroad tie arrangement. The angle of this walk is attractive and permits an efficient access to the home.

Arthur Rutenberg Homes by Lyons-Raffo Corp.

LOW-MAINTENANCE ENTRY—Pruning can be avoided by carefully selecting plants that never need it. Here contrast is created by the white liriope against the wall and the green juniper in the foreground.

Residence: Mr. and Mrs. Michael Kashtan

Y-SHAPED WALK—A Y-shaped entry walk, dressed in lots of low-growing shrubs, provides easy access from both directions. The hole in the roof will allow the palm growing in the courtyard to reach its full height in a few years.

U.S. Home, Rutenberg Div.

LOTS OF WALKING ROOM—For variety, a mounded, teardrop-shaped bed will lift the landscape. The shape of the bed follows the flow of the driveway, but is kept several feet from the drive to allow an unobstructed flow of foot traffic in and out of autos. The young trees are live oak (*Quercus virginiana*).

GOODNIGHT AREA—This outside foyer becomes the goodnight area with lights and potted plants. Well-selected and well-placed plants provided permanence with a funnel effect. See how your eye is drawn to the front door?

PINT-SIZED LANDSCAPE—This entry yard may be small but it packs a powerful visual punch. Notice the different textures in the wall, driveway, walkway, and by the door. All plants are low-maintenance and require little attention. Left to right are podocarpus, liriope, king sago palm, shore juniper, and cabbage palm.

ESTATE PLANNING—The spacious wooded lots of north Florida are often designed as estates with rolling green lawns dotted with specimen plants such as star magnolia (M. *stellata*), *Spirea van hootei*, redbud (*Cercis canadensis*), camellias and azaleas. The vine on the light post is Carolina jessamine (*Gelsemium sempervirens*) and displays fragrant yellow flowers each spring.

NATURAL HARMONY—ALL THAT'S NECESSARY—Hillside lots in Gainesville, cut from existing wooded areas, often have little landscaping other than foundation plants used to tie the home to the lot. Intensive landscaping in newly developed, bare earth subdivisions is necessary as a replacement for what we see in this view—a variety of textures on the ground and in the massive tree trunks, coupled with the natural harmony and sheltered feeling provided by the abundant native trees.

SHELTERED ENTRY—A *Phoenix reclinata* palm clump stands guard at this covered entryway. The trunks lean artistically toward the door while the fronds lightly shade the curved walkway.

MOBILE HOME ENTRY—Visitors move through an oasis of foliage to gain entry to this mobile home. Passage is via 20-inch popcorn stones set in marble chips. A large-leafed rubber plant (*Ficus elastica*) towers over an evergreen arborvitae. To the right is *Pittosporum tobira* and under the mailbox is a *Fatsia japonica*.

RAMP FOR WHEELCHAIR VISITORS—Team effort produced this island package. The landscape designer wanted wide steps, the thoughtful lady of the house wanted a wheelchair ramp that runs from the drive behind the island, the gentleman of the house wanted a small patio with benches, and the son wanted a basketball court (see the shadow of the backboard). This is a prime example of designer-owner teamwork.

Design: Mac Perry
Residence of Dr. and Mrs. Robert Burg, Seminole

THE PERFECT FRAME—The old Pass-a-Grille Community Church, converted to a home by interior designer Joan Haley, sports a thickly planted entry of cabbage palms (*Sabal palmetto*) that focuses attention where it belongs—on the front door. The columnar evergreens are Italian cypress (*Cupressus sempervirens*). The ground cover is shore juniper (*Juniperus conferta* 'Andersoni').

LAWN IS DRIVE—This handsome entry driveway is made of large concrete blocks set into Bermuda grass strips. The door is framed with mature schefflera and cereus cactus whose large flowers bloom on summer nights.

LIGHTS FOR BEAUTY AND FUNCTION—Ornamental lights like this wall hanger are great for augmenting the Spanish appeal of tile roofs so common in Florida. But eye-level lights block out the natural beauty of nightfall. Tiered lights lining the walkway provide better lighting for the path without destroying the beauty of the nighttime landscape.

BOLD ANNUALS LINE WALK—Colorful begonias that line this entry walkway can be planted from the first of March in north and central Florida and in October in south Florida. However, when hot weather arrives, they must be replaced with a summer annual. Try marigolds, dahlias, or phlox for summer beauty.

Design: William H. Roy, Landscape Architect

SWEEPING HEDGE—The strong "S" curve of this yaupon holly (*Ilex vomitoria* 'Nana') hedge catches the eye, swings it around the interestingly gnarled trunk of the *Ligustrum lucidum* tree, and brings it to rest at the front door.

SPRING HAS SPRUNG—North Florida landscapes burst into a blaze of color each spring when dogwoods, redbuds, azaleas, and camellias bloom. Notice the harmonious effect of the planted and native shrubbery framing this home.

WILDFLOWER ENTRANCE—To achieve the look of real wildflowers, plant common lantana near the entranceway. The red and yellow flowered one is L. *camara*. The attractive lilac variety is L. *montevidensis*. Be aware that frost will kill them in north Florida.

GOODNIGHT AREA—A small goodnight area is appropriately located halfway to the driveway, in the midst of landscape plantings and under the shelter of a pair of palms. A bench (or two) here might be a welcome addition.

U.S. Home, Rutenberg Div.

TRANSITIONAL WALL—Not only does this lamp light the path at night, but along with the brick wall it serves as a transitional feature to tie the landscape to the living room inside.

FRIENDLY BEGONIAS—Beautiful flowers such as these begonias express a welcome message at any home. The bottlebrush tree (*Callistemon citrinus*) provides vertical expression as it emerges from a bed of variegated pittosporum (*P. tobira* 'Variegatum').

TREE WITH DOUBLE ROLE—A stately *Ligustrum lucidum* tree is the focal point of this entranceway as seen from the door of the house. Its shade is enjoyed by a mass of azaleas encircled by eight-inch pilings that outline the walkway.

Arthur Rutenberg Homes by Lyons-Raffo Corp.

SHADED ENTRY—A specimen king sago palm (*Cycas revoluta*) greets visitors who approach this walkway. Shaded by a Ligustrum tree (*L. lucidum*), the bed is lined with poles that were treated to prevent wood rot and termites.

Arthur Rutenberg Homes by Lyons-Raffo Corp.

C H A P T E R

Six

TUB PLANTING—Small palms must be selected for urn and tub plantings. One of the best in south Florida is the solitaire palm (*Ptychosperma elegans*). These growing at Coconut Grove's Mayfair Mall are amidst a bed of blue *Plumbago capensis*. Prune plumbago heavily in late winter and it will exhibit flowers most of the year. White varieties are also available.

Ideas for commercial landscaping

Florida is experiencing a rapid growth of industrial complexes and commercial compounds. Perhaps this is due to the pull-power of such attractions as Walt Disney World, Busch Gardens, Cypress Gardens and Kennedy Space Center, or perhaps Americans simply seek to exchange snowstorms for sunshine.

With this growth we have the advent of city and regional environmental planning departments who assist landscape architects and designers to beautify commercial properties within the borders of public safety and environmental preservation. Considerations are given to water runoff, erosion, size and quantity of shade trees, choice of hardy plants and those providing shelter and food for birds, underground utilities, and a host of other guidelines.

By coordinating suggestions from the County Extension offices with these local agencies, businessmen, civic groups, and chambers of commerce now have opportunities to beautify their avenues, storefronts, and publicly owned properties. Consideration must be given to not blocking signs or traffic views and not significantly increasing public works landscape maintenance budgets. But even within these limits most Florida towns have wide opportunities for aesthetic improvement. Special opportunities are provided by the water retention ponds required on most commercial properties. As an example, these ponds can be planted with large colorful beds of canna in a plush green carpet lined with weeping willows. Many designers are locating miniparks by these ponds with picnic benches, shade trees, and pond fountains where employees can have their lunch.

Plants selected for commercial sites should be hardy against wind, cold, drought, and excess rain. These plants should be low-maintenance and relatively free of insects, diseases, and nematodes. There should be color pockets and beds large and flowing and filled with single varieties of shrubs to create a visual impact.

Mounds or earth swells should be subtle and not look like a buried elephant. Poor views of neighboring properties need to be blocked out and vistas framed for focalization.

And don't forget to go inside and look back through the windows to see the view from within. Landscape architect Phil Graham of St. Petersburg stands in a cherry picker bucket and is lifted up several stories where a high-rise condominium will be constructed to see what the view will be like from the fifth floor. Then he locates masses of tall palms to block out poor views and frame the pleasant views.

The UBS principle (unified, balanced, simplified) works as well on commercial landscapes as on residential plantings (see the introduction to Chapter Two). Unlike smaller, residential landscapes which are more attractive when they tie in to adjacent neighborhood landscapes by using similar plants and lines, commercial properties are usually large enough to stand on their own, giving the designer more freedom.

Most landscape designers make a condominium complex or commercial setting into a microworld set apart from the rest of the community—an oasis in the desert, where residents and shoppers can retreat to a garden of Eden. Producing this effect requires completely surrounding barriers, such as an immense hedgerow of oaks, as well as lots of green lawn and an especially attractive entrance road enhanced with sculpture and colorful flowers changed periodically.

Following is a selection of commercial landscapes to help stimulate your own creativity.

NATURAL APPEARANCE—Commercial entrances densely planted like this take on a natural flow when shorter varieties are planted to the front backdropped by tall specimens. Tall palms are Chinese fan palms (*Livistona chinensis*). Screw pine (*Pandanus utilis*) is at the lower right.

SKYSCAPING—Along Miami's Bay Shore Drive overlooking Key Biscayne Island and the sparkling Atlantic stands a magnificent display of landscaped architecture. The Grand Bay Hotel lifts giant planter boxes of clusia and colorful bougainvillea high into the sky.

PLANTER BOX PARADE—This handsome planter box contains a superb blend of textures in cascade and accent plants. All of these plants are low-maintenance and require little pruning. The large plant in the center is screw pine (*Pandanus utilis*). *Asparagus sprengeri* spills over the wall.

Grand Bay Hotel—Miami

GETTING DOWN TO BUSINESS—The facade and entry of this office building was designed by its landscape architect owner Jim Voss. Emerging from a nest of fishtail ferns is *Pongamia pinnata*, the pongam tree. Its springtime, pinkish-white, pea-type flowers are followed by 1½"-long poisonous pods with beaklike points. For foundation shrubbery Jim chose the colorful *Ixora coccinea* 'Nora Grant,' and on both sides of the entry door, *Schefflera arboricola*.

SCULPTURE DEFINES ENTRY—The entrance to this industrial compound is marked by a handsome industrial-appearing sculpture by Robbie Robinson of Indian Rocks Beach. Lacing the bottom are colorful, eye-stopping petunias that bloom all fall, winter, and spring.

Rubin-Pinellas Center for Commerce and Industry—Largo

SOLID SCULPTURE—Modern sculptures like this are becoming commonplace at public buildings and industrial complexes. They are a sign of a modern, educated society. This one suggests stability with its simple, balanced, geometric steel forms— the triangle, rectangle, square, circle. Stop and discover its qualities. That's what sculpture is all about.

WELL-DRESSED OFFICE ENTRY

THE APPROACH—Approaching this office building there is just enough lawn to accent the flow of the bed of *Liriope muscari*. The bottlebrush shrub (*Callistemon rigidus*) on the left will be kept small while its cousin the bottlebrush tree (*Callistemon citrinus*) on the right will grow to 20 feet to cover the bare wall. In the background a *Cocos plumosa* palm (*Syagrus romanzoffianum*) dances in the breeze.

Rubin-Pinellas Center for Commerce and Industry—Largo

THE ENTRY—Framing the symmetrically balanced entry is *Asparagus sprengeri* ground cover, a couple of hardy king sago palms (*Cycas revoluta*), and a pair of delicate pink La France hibiscus standards. North Florida landscapers might choose azalea standards or camellias.

Rubin-Pinellas Center for Commerce and Industry—Largo

WORKING WITH EXISTING CONDITIONS—This entrance to the Rubin Pinellas Center for Commerce and Industry is marked with a large laurel oak (*Quercus laurifolia*) that existed before the complex was built. Bright night lights lighten not only the sign but also the handsome tree.

EYE CATCHER—Brilliant gold chrysanthemums that have a long blooming season are massed at the entry to this condominium in Pasadena. They catch and hold the eye for several blocks. A large clump of *Phoenix reclinata* palms provides a sheltered effect but is placed well behind the name so as not to hide it.

JMC Communities, Inc.—St. Petersburg

ABSTRACT PALMS—If landscape design is defined as the development of outdoor space for beauty and usage, then it includes this abstract wall design that echoes the angle of nearby cabbage palm (*Sabal palmetto*) trunks.

Rubin-Pinellas Center for Commerce and Industry—Largo

LANDSCAPING COMMERCIAL COMPLEXES—All over the state commercial complexes are springing up like wildflowers to match the immigration of industry seeking a warmer climate. To serve as an example of good landscaping for these complexes I have chosen the Rubin Bryan Dairy Center for Commerce and Industry in Largo. The landscape architect was William H. Roy, Clearwater. Here you see examples of entries, roadways, parking lots, and retention pond plantings.

WHIRLING WHEELS OF COMMERCE—At the entrance the whirling wheels of American business are announced by Palm Harbor sculptor Ken Edwards as his work silhouettes against a silver-lined sky.

LOW MAINTENANCE AND COLOR—Just inside, the entry road is lighted and landscaped with planter pockets designed for low maintenance and color. To the left, the yellow of 'Howardi' ligustrum provides a base for the spring flowering bottlebrush tree. Foreground bed holds 'Wheeleri' pittosporum and standard oleander shrubs pruned into small trees.

MEDIAN STRIP PLANTINGS—Farther along are variations of bed shapes and plant species to present variety. But desired low-maintenance and color are retained. Here the ground cover is hardy, variegated *Pittosporum tobira*. In place of the weeping bottlebrush, northern designers might use dogwood or redbud.

PARKING LOT BORDER—Flowing lines in this border planting are created with creosoted poles that hold back low-maintenance shrub masses of colorful, yellow-leafed Ligustrum 'Howardi' and a bed of variegated *Pittosporum tobira* surrounding a Canary Island date palm (*Phoenix canariensis*).

RIVERBANK WILLOWS—Gracious weeping willows were planted around the huge retention lake. The geyser fountain adds not only sight and sound pleasure but stirs the surface to reduce stagnating growth in the water.

OASIS IN CONCRETE JUNGLE—The huge parking lot adjacent to the industrial complex is framed by an oasis planting of *Cocos plumosa* palms (*Syagrus romanzoffianum*) whose lacey fronds sway in the slightest breeze. Hardy *Pittosporum tobira* massed at their base require very little care. Notice how the undulating shape of the beds adds movement to the landscape.

STYLISH DRAINAGE GRATES—To insure that this 'East Palatka' holly (*Ilex opaca*) receives plenty of water, a handsome drainage grate has been worked into the design of the sidewalk. Its framing brickwork echoes the arches of the building's windows.

HOME CONVERTED TO OFFICE

VENERABLE TWO-STORY—This St. Petersburg residence has been completely remodeled in a theme reminiscent of Southern living by the owners, landscape architect Phil Graham and his wife Stephanie, who presently use it for their office. The large pots of flowering periwinkle (*Vinca spp.*) and the tile spilling down to the street fashionably greet their clients. The low-maintenance aluminum fence is softened with hedge plantings of Japanese boxwood (*Buxus microphylla*).

SIGHT AND SOUND—A small ceramic frog recycles water into the pond to add soft sound to the visual joy of this postage stamp-sized landscape. The aquatic plant is umbrella plant (*Cyperus alternifolius*), which is related to papyrus. The shiny, dense ground cover on the left is the little-leaf Confederate jasmine (*Trachelospermum jasminoides*).

CACTUS MEDIAN—Along the busy thoroughfare of South Pasadena on Florida's Suncoast can be seen this low-maintenance succulent garden of a wide assortment of arid zone plants growing through a mulched bed of earthy cinders.

A PARKSIDE PLAN—What makes this St. Petersburg parkside idea unique—besides plenty of seating on comfortable benches, a trash receptacle, and colorful flowers—is the horseshoe sidewalk that separates the sitters from the main flow of traffic.

PSYCHOLOGICALLY DESIGNED WALK—Somehow walkways become far less restraining when an island planting provides opportunity for you to walk left or right. You are given a choice and where you walk becomes your decision, not the designer's.

RACE TO THE SKY—Creeping fig (*Ficus pumila*) grows from planters conveniently tucked behind huge, splashy fountains. They creep up the brick columns and race skyward on the face of the Tampa City Hall complex.

POOLSIDE PLANTING—Providing an enclosing background for this Tallahassee pool is a king sago palm (*Cycas revoluta*) on the left surrounded by a specimen lady palm (*Rhapis excelsa*), and nearby, a towering *Magnolia grandiflora*. Poolside plantings should be broadleaf evergreens that do not lose their leaves into the pool during dormant seasons. This hardy collection thrives in north Florida while retaining the flavor of tropical south Florida.

MINI-GARDEN—Just outside this office window is a tiny pocket of soil large enough for a pleasant planting of lady palms (*Rhapis excelsa*), crotons, and small liriope. To the busy worker inside it provides a glancing relief from the humdrum paperwork.

Design: Phil Graham and Company, St. Petersburg

AESTHETIC BALANCE—Here is a good example of the aesthetic concept of mass-space-mass, with the space at eye level permitting a clear view of the spherical fan fountain. The ground cover shrub is *Ilex vomitoria*. The handsomely pruned tree is *Ligustrum lucidum*.

TALLAHASSEE OFFICE PLANTING—Here is a hardy combo that would take a four-inch snow load if we had one. Intense green Chinese holly (*Ilex cornuta*) shows its prickly leaves at the ground level. Darker-colored yaupon holly (*Ilex vomitoria*) is in the planter. A Pfitzer juniper (*Juniperus chinensis* 'Pfitzeriana') sprawls at the corner next to a creeping fig vine (*Ficus pumila*). And between the windows is heavenly bamboo (*Nandina domestica*) whose foliage and berries turn red-orange in the fall. All these plants are low-maintenance and very hardy for typical north Florida climates.

A QUIET RETREAT—Just steps away from a noisy, downtown street is this peaceful, shaded pocket to provide a moment's rest for tired shoppers.

COLONIAL BRICK RAISED PLANTER—In the entry court of this refurbished old firehouse, the arched pattern continues in a raised planter bed containing *Vinca minor* along its edge, with 'low dense' pyracantha and 'East Palatka' (*Ilex opaca*) holly trees at its center.

Phil Graham, Landscape Architect

A SHADY RETREAT—In the quaint Coconut Grove community of south Miami, black olives (*Bucida buceras*) line the streets shading sidewalk cafes. These 40-foot, south Florida trees are salt-tolerant, require no maintenance, and remain unchanged throughout the year.

AVENUE TREES

Trees planted along the streets and avenues of Florida must meet certain restrictions. They can't be fast-growing and brittle, they mustn't get too tall, they should retain their leaves year-round or at least not be too messy. Their roots must go deep and not break up concrete, they must be low-maintenance and relatively pest-resistant, and their appearance must be architecturally sound, conforming to the structure of buildings and streets. Many municipalities offer a list of such trees.

Their use on city streets is to soften the stiff architectural lines of building structures, provide cooling shade in an otherwise concrete jungle, filter out dust and smog, deaden sound, and if possible offer some variety to the routine of city life with an occasional burst of showy flowers.

NEEDS LOTS OF SPACE—Lining the median of Highway One in Miami's Coral Gables are splendid specimens of *Harpullia arobria*. And dangling from their branches are interesting, double-fruited red berries. Notice how the lower branches have been pruned away to avoid contact with trucks and buses.

BURST OF GOLD—Silver trumpet tree or *Tabebuia argentia* explodes with flowers of gold along silver branches in spring. Its short height makes it a good choice for avenue or patio trees in south Florida. Central Florida might substitute Jerusalem thorn (*Parkinsonia aculeata*) and for north Florida, dogwood (*Cornus florida*).

A WEEPING OASIS—Weeping bottlebrush (*Callistemon citrinus*), 20-foot lacy trees with bold, red spikes of flowers in spring, cast heavy shade for resting cyclers and strollers at this sidewalk retreat in Coconut Grove. Citrus-smelling leaves remain year-round.

STURDY TREE WITH VARIETY—The mahogany (*Swietenia mahogani*) is planted 30 feet apart in south Florida to provide a stout avenue tree that holds strong in storms, doesn't cast so dense a shade that other plants can't grow under it, and for variety drops its leaves in winter to silhouette its skeletal branches against the sky.

STOREFRONT PLANTINGS—The rapid growth of ear leaf acacia (*Acacia auriculaeformis*) makes it popular, but it must be protected from high winds as it is brittle. Abundant clusters of yellow flowers appear in early spring on these 25-foot trees growing in Palm Beach. Great for small shops and mildly salt-tolerant.

TUNNEL OF MAJESTY—Only in the jungle city, Miami, can you find such majestic displays of ficus trees as these. In cooler portions of the state they freeze back every few years and are not worth it. The vigorous surface roots tend to lift the street if not given plenty of room.

AVENUE PALMS

Often palms are selected for avenue plantings. They have the disadvantage of not serving as a dust and noise filter and they cast little shade. But they have the advantage of a small root system and thrive with very little water. In many species if the spathe is cut before the flowers open you avoid the bee-attracting stage and the numerous petals and fruits that fall to the ground. In south Florida, watch for falling coconuts! North Florida avenues must be planted with hardier species such as the tall *Washingtonia robusta*, or our state tree the cabbage palm (*Sabal palmetto*), or where space permits the wide and stately Canary Island date palm (*Phoenix canariensis*).

Here are a few good examples of avenue palms used in the warmer parts of Florida.

THE VERSATILE COCONUT—One of south Florida's favorite palms is the coconut. Young specimens have arching trunks giving them a wind-blown, tropical look. Medium palms seen here on the campus of the University of Miami have thick, graceful heads and begin to bear edible coconuts. Tall palms up to 60 feet are highly salt-tolerant and withstand the intense light and heat of Florida's southern peninsula.

PALMS OF REGALRY—Perhaps the most stately palm of all is the royal palm (*Roystonea spp.*) with its sturdy, straight trunk that exhibits a smooth and shiny green crownshaft for several feet under the pinnate-leafed head. These closely planted specimens are along Fort Myers' McGregor Boulevard near the home of Thomas Edison.

PALMS FOR MOBILE HOME PARK—Young *Cocos plumosa* palms (*Syagrus romanzoffianum*) line a mobile home street in Orlando. These "queen palms" are the most popular palm of central Florida due to their low cost, availability, and graceful beauty. The lacey fronds sway in even the slightest breeze.

C H A P T E R

Seven

Grassless landscape displays array of tropical foliage plants often sold as house plants. Overhead trees shade and protect. Lower left, tree fern. Upper left, lady palm (*Rhapis excelsa*). Upper right, *Philodendron selloum*.

Selecting the correct plant

This important reference chapter will help you choose the right plant for every situation. A mistake in plant selection, even after making a good design and properly preparing plant beds, ultimately will destroy the overall landscape scheme. An incorrect plant selection could disrupt the landscape's beauty, nullify its usefulness, or demand increased maintenance, with the result that even the most avid gardener will eventually give up on the plan.

FACTORS TO CONSIDER

In the planning stage of a landscape, it is always better to think in terms of size, shape, color, and texture rather than specific plants. Say, "I'll need a large barrier here to block out that poor view. Something tall there to shade the patio in the afternoon. And here by the door there should be a low border to sweep around a three- or four-foot mass planting of something colorful under those windows." Get the idea? Don't get bogged down with trying to name plants in the design stage.

Once you have a pretty good idea about desired sizes and shapes, consider the following factors:

1. **Hardiness**—This factor usually refers to a plant's ability to withstand cold. Damage comes in three ways: *Freezing temperatures* cause plant fluids to expand and burst the cells in the leaves and fruit, leaving them lifeless. *Frost* can settle on exposed leaves in the chill just before dawn. *Cold winds* knock the leaves off many semi-deciduous species leaving them bare until spring.

Plants can be protected by covering them with sheets, blankets, or large cardboard boxes on cold nights.

Many plants that will survive temperatures below the twenties up north can freeze in Florida at 28 or 30 degrees. Up north it gets cold gradually, forcing plants into a protective dormancy. Then it stays cold all winter. In Florida, I've seen December and January temperatures in the fifties for several days which then plunge to 30 degrees for a couple of nights. Cold-hardy shrubs such as ligustrum and euonymus aren't prepared for this abuse and suffer cold more here than in Virginia.

In general selecting *native* plants indigenous to Florida is the best choice. Even if they get "burned" (frostbitten) occasionally, they are less likely to die.

2. **Water requirements**—Many plants including ligustrum, citrus, podocarpus, and schefflera suffer during Florida's rainy summer months. Ask your nurseryman about water requirements when you consider plants. Avoid grouping plants which prefer damp soils with those which like dry soil unless the dry plants are mounded up and have extra sand added to their soil mix to allow for drainage. Also, unless the species can handle extreme conditions, avoid placing plants under the eave of a roof where the soil stays relatively dry or next to a down spout where the ground gets flooded.

3. **Soil requirements**—Azalea, ixora, camellia, and gardenia like an acid soil and an acid fertilizer. Avoid planting them in alkaline soils or with plants preferring alkaline soil. Most plants like a soil pH between 5.5 and 6.5. The acid-lovers do better at pH 4.5 to 6.0. Purchase an inexpensive pH test kit from local garden shops to test your soil. Most Florida plants like the soil loose and airy, with the ability to retain moisture. Mixing sand and peat with your potting soil will give you both.

Fertility is a consideration, too. Nasturtium and geraniums bloom better in a soil low in nutrients. Therefore, avoid planting them with roses or philodendron which do better in rich soils. Soil pH, texture, moisture and fertility are all factors to consider when choosing plants.

4. **Light requirements**—A bright, sunny day in Florida will produce nearly 12,000 foot-candles of light. Many plants like this. But many others do not. The tropicals that grow naturally under a jungle canopy do better in the shade where foot-candles rarely reach 5,000. [Note: Light requirements are so important that I've included them with each plant listed in the alphabetical lists in this chapter.]

5. **Salt tolerance**—With so many of Florida's cities nestled along its coast, salt tolerance becomes an important consideration, too. Some plants, such as oleander,* shore juniper, Australian pine,* and sea hibiscus, can take the abuse of salty soil and seaside conditions that spray plants daily with a misty sea breeze. Other plants can withstand mild salt drift, when they are planted a block or two away from the shore. Still others won't tolerate salt in the air or soil. At the end of this chapter I've included a helpful list of salt-tolerant plants.

6. **Pest resistance**—Some plants seem to have a natural attraction to plant pests. Chewing caterpillars just love oleander, oaks, canna, and hibiscus leaves; piercing-sucking pests such as scales, white flies, and aphids not only suck plant juices but their honeydew droppings cause a black sooty-mold fungus to grow on the leaves of such plants as citrus, ixora, India hawthorn, gardenia, and bishop wood; thrips infect crotons and cause Cuban laurel leaves to curl; tiny mites feed on leaves of croton, pyracantha, and many evergreens, especially Italia cypress; leaf diseases are frequently seen on pittosporum, laurel oaks, roses, crape myrtle, and ligustrum; borers get in the wood of oaks, pines, and maples; root rots are often found in azaleas, jacarandas, and viburnum; nematodes are common on annuals and vegetables, mandevilla, and on ungrafted gardenia, citrus, and roses; and the list goes on. With so many pests in the Florida environment, home landscapers would be wise to select as many plants as possible that have a natural resistance to these invaders, such as those listed in the native plant list at the end of this chapter.

7. **Physical requirements**—These considerations include the ultimate sizes and shapes of plants, as well as their textures, whether prickly, spiney, large-leafed, soft, or smooth. Year-round interest needs to be considered, too. Choosing plants that bloom in succession so the landscape will have color all year-round is a rewarding task. Also, fresh spring leaves, buds, fruit, fall color, and

seed pods can provide interest just as well as flowers.

I have found it easier when choosing plants to think in terms of the floors, walls and ceilings of a landscape. Floors are grass lawns, ground covers, shrubs (under one foot in height), patios, walkways, and driveways. Walls are hedges, shrub borders, fences, actual walls, and accent plants (up to about ten feet). Ceilings are large trees (that cast shade and protect against settling frost), open patio roofs, arbors, and overhead trellises.

With so many preliminary factors to consider before choosing plants, you can easily see why designers avoid cluttering their thoughts with plant selection during the early design stage. Plant selection should be the last stage in landscape design.

PLANT ZONES

Florida is such a long and narrow state that its plant life changes through three zones. In the northern portion of the state the plant life is much like that found throughout other southeastern states. All four seasons are distinct. Winters are cold and bare. With spring comes the burst of wisteria, dogwood, redbud, azaleas, and camellias. Summers are pleasantly warm and autumn puts red and gold in maple leaves.

Central Florida is a testing ground for the tropicals of south Florida. Many adapt well—others don't. But in central Florida there is a fortunate blending of the temperate and tropical plants giving designers a vast array of plant choices. Central Florida is about as far south as you'll see redbuds and dogwoods. It is also about as far north as you'll see poinciana and the Florida orchid tree. Winters in central Florida are lovely and mild but there are usually three or four nights a year when a freeze occurs and tender plants will need protection.

South Florida is unique to our country. With its humid, nonfreezing winters, landscape designers have a heyday planting the colorfully leafed, large-flowered plants of the Caribbean. Exotic edible fruits, such as carambola, coconut, and lychee, are commonplace. Unusual "curiosity" plants, such as the sausage tree* and the shaving brush tree, provide interest. Other southern states with nonfreezing temperatures—Texas, Arizona, New Mexico—have arid climates. They grow lots of cacti and succulents, but the jungle plants belong to south Florida. Following Cutler Road along the shore in southeast Miami you get the feeling you're on a trail blazed out of a dense jungle—in fact, you are. The twisted boughs of ficus trees slowly stretch to surround you, while their roots tear at the soil under the road.

In order to keep the three zones distinct and thereby minimize plant death, nurserymen and landscape designers use a zone map to divide the state into its north, central and south plant zones.

PLANTS FOR FLORIDA LANDSCAPES

Following are descriptions of over 300 plants categorized according to their landscape usage.

Zone map for Florida landscapes

N = Northern Florida
C = Central Florida
S = Southern Florida

Ajuga (A. *reptans rubra*) or bugleweed, a ground cover carpet.

Artillery plant (*Pilea microphylla*).

Billbergia spp., an air plant in the Bromeliaceae family.

GROUND COVERS

NCS = planting zone
S-Sh = prefers sun or shade
* = photo

The following plants grow less than two feet tall unless noted otherwise. They show best when planted in masses or as borders in front of taller shrubs or trees. Those pictured in a nearby photo are marked *

1. **Alternanthera** (*Alternanthera* spp.)   CS, S-Sh

Dense little shrub with small leaves displaying various shades of red, orange, or lavender. Good for borders around shrub beds with dark green or white leaves. Space 18 inches.

2. **Ajuga or Bugleweed** (A. *reptans rubra*)*   NCS, Sh

Makes a thick mass of three-inch cover, displaying bronze, two-inch leaves. Bugleweed is very common in northwestern Florida where it covers large banks, slopes, and parkways. Prefers well-drained, fertile soil, but dislikes hot, sandy soils. Space 18 inches.

3. **Artillery plant** (*Pilea microphylla*)*   CS, S-Sh

A succulent herb about a foot tall with tiny, nearly white leaves. Mass around boulders for a rock garden effect. Mow every five years for best appearance. Space 12 inches.

4. **Begonia** (B. *semperflorens*)   CS, Sh

Wax begonias are popular fall, winter and spring flowers displaying blooms of white, pink, or red. Leaves are green or bronze-to-purple and add extra color as a border plant. Great for hanging baskets, too. Space 12 inches.

5. **Billbergia** (*Billbergia* spp.)*   CS, S-Sh

These favorites of the Bromeliad family (which includes pineapple) make good rock garden plants or massed growths around the base of a tree. Most display spectacular spikes of flowers in early fall. Easy to grow. Space 18 inches.

6. **Crown of thorns** (*Euphorbia milii*)   CS, S

Cousin to the poinsettia. Its thick, thorny stems contain milky sap and support clusters of tiny pink or red flowers. Its thorns restrict the movement of dogs, possums or other creatures who overturn your garbage cans. Space 18 inches.

7. **Cuphea** (C. *hyssopifolia*)   CS, S-Sh

A dwarf leafy shrub that shows off its tiny flowers of white, pale pink, or lavender throughout much of year. Water during dry periods. Use for borders or bunched. Space 18 inches

8. **Day lily** (*Hemerocallis* spp.)*   NCS, S-Sh

Easy to grow. Add manure and peat to its soil. Day lilies produce many short-lived flowers in yellow and orange. Divide clumps in winter and plant in masses 18 inches apart. Tall varieties produce three- to four-foot stalks.

Perennial day lilies dance beneath colorful crape myrtles

Ivy (*Hedera* spp.) makes dense, hardy ground cover.

White-leaved *Ligustrum sinensis* framed in a bed of dwarf juniper (*Juniperus* spp.). Creosote post edging wired for rigidity.

224

9. Ferns   NCS, Sh

Florida has a number of native ferns that make good ground covers. House holly fern, leather leaf fern and Boston fern are three common ones. Plant divided plants in wooded locations about 18 inches apart.

10. Ivy (*Hedera* spp.)*   NCS, Sh

Clinging tendrils make the ivies a popular vine as well as ground cover. English ivy (H. *helix*) and Algerian ivy (H. *canariensis*) with its larger leaf and salt tolerance are two of the most popular. Plant 24 inches apart in well-drained soil.

11. Jasmine, dwarf Confederate (*Trachelospermum jasminoides* 'Microphylla')   NCS, S-Sh

This tiny-leafed version of Confederate jasmine (which also is a good ground cover) covers the ground quickly in a dense mat. Don't plant under shrubs; jasmine will climb and smother nearby plants. For good effect, let jasmine spill over a retaining wall. Space 24 inches.

12. Juniper (*Juniperus* spp.) *   NCS, S

A number of low, spreading junipers offering high-quality appearance are available: shore juniper (J. *conferta*) and its highly salt-tolerant variety 'Andersoni,' and several cultivars of J. *horizontalis*—'Bar Harbor,' 'Blue Rug,' and 'Douglasii' with its steel blue foliage, popular in north Florida. Plant 30 inches apart.

13. Lantana (L. *montevidensis*)   CS, S-Sh

Weeping Lantana is a low, vinelike shrub with rosy-lilac flowers borne in clusters almost year-round. Space 24 inches.

14. Liriope (*Liriope* spp.)*   NCS, S-Sh

Species of lily turf; ranges from six inches to two feet, with a dense, broadleaf grass appearance. Purplish flowers are borne on spikes in summer. Mildly salt-tolerant. Space 12 inches.

15. Mondo grass (*Ophiopogon japonicus*)

NCS, S-Sh

For a finer texture and shorter plant (than liriope) use this dainty cover as a border to outline your plant beds. Mildly salt-tolerant. Space divided plants a few inches apart.

16. Oyster plant (*Rhoeo discolor*)*   CS, S-Sh

Moses-in-the-bulrushes has tall, wide lance-shaped leaves of purple and green for a rich color accent. Will not withstand foot traffic. Space 12 inches.

17. Pepperomia (*Pepperomia* spp.)   S, Sh

This popular, American house plant makes an impressive ground cover in south Florida where its numerous cultivars grace shaded locations. Glossy, dark green leaves about three inches in diameter. Space 12 inches.

18. Pittosporum (P. *tobira* 'Wheeleri')

NCS, S-Sh

The 'Wheeleri' pittosporum is a dense, low variety of its popular parent. Protect against scales and leaf spot disease. Space 24 inches. Green thumb-shaped leaves cover shrub in a tight mass.

19. **Purple queen** (*Setcreasea purpurea*)*
CS, S-Sh

The purple stems of this herbaceous perennial creep along the ground; its six-inch purple leaves point upward for bright color contrast to surroundings. Not a dense cover. Space 12 inches.

20. **Periwinkle** (*Vinca minor*)   NC, S-Sh

Glossy, heart-shaped leaves and profuse flowers of pink, white or red (in summer) make this one of the most colorful, easy-to-grow ground covers. Space 24 inches in any soil.

21. **Rose moss** (*Portulaca* spp.)   NCS, S

A colorfully flowered succulent that thrives in hot, dry locations. Flowers close in the afternoon. Space 12 inches.

22. **Society garlic** (*Tulbaghia violacea*) NCS, S-Sh

Growing in tall, grasslike clumps, this herbaceous perennial produces purple flowers on two-foot spikes during warm months. Plant 12 inches apart.

23. **Spider plant** (*Chlorophytum comosum*)CS, Sh

This popular hanging basket plant displays long, green and white "spiders" at the ends of its threadlike stems; can withstand a light freeze and could be used more often as a ground cover.

24. **Springeri fern** (*Asparagus sprengeri*)
NCS, S-Sh

Small feathery shrub that looks like a fern, but isn't. Likes moist, fertile soil, but is easy to grow anywhere. Its yellow-green appearance makes it a nice contrast for blue-green or dark green plants. Space 30 inches to allow plenty of room to spread.

25. **Wandering Jew** (*Zebrina pendula*)   CS, Sh

A creeping, succulent perennial in tones of purple, silver, and green. Likes rich soil. Makes a good rock garden plant. Space rooted cuttings a few inches apart.

26. **Wedelia** (*Wedelia trilobata*)   NCS, S-Sh

A dense-growing, bright green, creeping perennial with yellow flowers (during warm months). Roots and grows easily in almost any soil. Give plenty of room to creep. Use on slopes, spilling over walls, around rocks or taller plants, near seaside. Space rooted cuttings several inches apart.

27. **Winter creeper** (*Euonymus fortunei*) N, S-Sh

Dull green leaves with whitish veins on a low, evergreen shrub. Creeps over a large area or climbs to 20 feet. Shear periodically. Silver-edged and bronze varieties available. Likes moist, fertile, acid soils. Space 12 inches.

Giant clumps of *Liriope* displayed on a mound of soil for better show.

Oyster plant (*Rhoeo discolor*).

Purple queen (*Setcreasea purpurea*) ground cover.

Angel's trumpet (*Datura* spp.) dangles magnificent white trumpets.

Weeping or citrus-leaved bottlebrush (*Callistemon citrinus*) sits in a bed of well-pruned variegated pittosporum (*Pittosporum tobira*).

SHRUBS WITH SHOWY COLOR

NCS = planting zone
S-Sh = prefers sun or shade
6'-12' = heights commonly seen
* = photo

Most shrubs around the home are planted from three to four feet apart. Many listed here have showy flowers part of the year to add seasonal change. Others have colorful foliage all year. Colorful shrubs usually look best when planted in clusters in front of tall barrier plants or massed around taller trees.

1. **Abelia** (A. *grandiflora*) N, S-Sh, 4'-10'
Shiny green leaves on reddish twigs holding white tubular flowers with red calyces. Abelia makes a distinctive foundation plant or, in clumps, an informal screen. Likes rich, clay-loam soils.

2. **Allamanda** (A. *cathartica*) CS, S, 2'-8'
Large, yellow, trumpet flowers throughout the warm season are distinct. May be trained as a vine. A brown-bud variety and purple-flower variety (A. *violacea*) are also popular. Grow in a planter or on a trellis.

3. **Angel's trumpet** (D*atura* spp.)*
CS, S-Sh, 10'-13'
Several species of this large, bushy shrub produce spectacular, hanging, white trumpet flowers up to twelve inches in summer. Fragrant. Plant to rear where it can tower over smaller shrubs. All parts of this plant are toxic.

4. **Azalea** (R*hododendron* spp.) NC, S-Sh, 1'-10'
Numerous varieties available in white, pink, red, purple, yellow, and orange. Profuse blossoms in spring. Dwarfs and giants available. (Ask your nurseryman for desired heights and spacing.) Prefers moist, acid soils. Plant shallow and mulch.

5. **Bottlebrush** (C*allistemon rigidus*)*
NCS, S, 6'-12'
Red bottlebrush-like flowers in springs. Thin shrub with narrow leaves. Easy to grow in well-drained soils.

6. **Bougainvillea** (B*ougainvillea* spp.)
CS, S, 6'-15'
Can be pruned to a shrub or tied to a trellis to support growth as a vine (to 30 feet if desired). Produces brilliant flower bracts in red, magenta, white, orange, and purple varieties. Train on top of a wall or arbor for a Spanish look. Beware of thorns.

7. **Camellia** (C. *japonica*) NC, S-Sh, 6'-12'
Popular belle of the old South often grown in a special garden (as are roses) where late winter flowers in red, white, and striped or blotched can be enjoyed. Likes acid soils. Spray for tea scale under older leaves.

8. Canna (*Canna* spp.)   NCS, S, 3'-5'

Giant flower clusters displayed in yellow, white, red, pink, and cream are popular in many summer gardens. Plant rhizomes (bulb-like structures) two inches deep in rich, moist soil. Spray giant, oval leaves for leaf roller caterpillars.

9. Cassia (*Cassia* spp.)   NCS, S, 10'-15'

Feathery oval leaves containing numerous leaflets on large, upright shrubs; may freeze to the ground. C. *bicapsularis* has yellow butterfly flowers in the winter. C. *alata* produces fat, yellow, upright candles in the fall. Both are quite attractive. Spray for caterpillars in the fall.

10. Chenille (*Acalypha hispida*)   S, S, 6'-8'

Dense shrub that dangles showy red cattails (16" long) for a real curiosity piece in the warmest months. Prune as needed and plant in well-drained soil.

11. Clusia (*C. rosea*)   S, S-Sh, 10'-20'

Thick, leathery leaves (4 x 8 inches) and clusters of showy white or pink flowers. Often espaliered in south Florida. Variegated species available. Called pitch apple because of its prominent three-inch fruit that splits to display seeds at maturity.

12. Copper plant (*Acalypha wilkesiana*)
CS, S, 6'-12'

Very colorful red to purple leaves year-round on a dense sprawling shrub. Bold when placed against a white wall or behind white- to yellow-leafed shrubs. Cold winds may defoliate.

13. Croton (*Codiaeum variegatum*) CS, S-Sh, 4'-8'

Large leaves, some twisted, in blends of red, yellow, and orange make this the most colorful shrub in Florida. Good for year-long interest. Many varieties and leaf shapes to choose from.

14. Dombeya (*D. wallichii*)   CS, S-Sh, 10'-20'

Tall, upright canes bear large, heart-shaped leaves. In winter large balls of pink flowers dangle on the foot-long stems of this curiosity plant. Perhaps too sparse to consider as serious, permanent, planting.

15. Downy myrtle (*Rhodomyrtus tomentosa*)
S, S-Sh, 6'-8'

Wooly gray-green leaves, attractive clusters of pink blossoms in warmer months, and downy, purple berries prized for pies and jellies make this a popular south Florida specimen.

16. Firecracker bush (*Russelia equisetiformis*)
S, S-Sh, 3'-6'

For best display, plant where long, weeping stems, displaying tiny leaves and dozens of red flowers, can cascade over a retaining wall. Growth appears dense and feathery.

Oleander (*Nerium oleander*) produces bloom all summer long.

Female varieties of pampas grass (*Cortaderia* spp.) have the most feathery plumes.

17. Gardenia (G. *jasminoides*)   NCS, S-Sh, 3'-6'
Famed Southern shrub with deliciously fragrant white to yellow flowers in the spring. Shiny leaves need spraying to combat sucking insects. Central and south Florida landscapers should plant only grafted plants to protect against nematodes. Prefers acid soils.

18. Hibiscus (H. *rosa-sinensis*)   CS, S-Sh, 6'-12'
Hundreds of single and double varieties grafted and grown for their colorful flowers in an array of colors. Used as hedge, screen, specimen, or cluster. Slightly acid, moist, and fertile soil preferred.

19. Hydrangea (H. *macrophylla*)   NC, Sh, 3'-4'
Coarse-textured, large-leaf shrub produces pink snowball flowers on alkaline soils, blue clusters on acid soils. Likes fertile, well-drained soil. White flowers indicate neutral soil.

20. Ixora (I. *coccinea*)   CS, S, 4'-12'
Easily cold-damaged but the profusion of red, yellow, or orange flower clusters throughout the warmer months makes ixora one of the most colorful flowering shrubs. Likes rich, acidic, well-drained soils.

21. Jacobina (Jacobina spp.)   CS, Sh, 3'-6'
Large, wavy leaves on a dense shrub. Produces terminal clusters of curved flower petals in late summer. Many colors available. Prefers well-drained, moderately rich soil.

22. Jasmine (Jasminum spp.)   NCS, S, 2'-10'
A number of species and sizes exist. Most are low, viny shrubs that can be trained on a trellis or as a low shrub. Its small white flowers are not too showy. Primrose jasmine of north and central Florida is yellow. Easy to grow.

23. Ligustrum (Ligustrum spp.)   NCS, S, 4'-8'
Two varieties are colorful. The variegated L. *lucidum* varieties have yellow-tipped leaves and the small-leafed privet, L. *sinensis*, has white leaves. Both make excellent contrast plantings for year-round interest. Well-drained soils are best.

24. Oleander (Nerium oleander)*   NCS, S, 6'-12'
A long, profuse blooming season, bold flower clusters in white, pink, and reds, plus a very high salt tolerance and drought resistance make this one of Florida's most popular flowering shrubs. Dwarf varieties are available but flowers are not as bold. Spray for caterpillars.

25. Pampas grass (Cortaderia selloana)*
NCS, S, 6'-8'
Tall, white feathery plumes tower over a four-foot clump of perennial grass late in season. Flower stalks can be cut before they are fully developed and dried for indoor display. Grass clumps may be cut to one foot before spring flush of flowers. Propagate by division.

26. **Plumbago, blue** (P. *capensis*)*   CS, S, 3'-6'

This shrub with its small, light blue, pinwheel flowers blooms profusely mainly in the warmer months. May be trained as a vine to cover a wire fence. Dislikes alkaline soils.

27. **Poinsettia** (*Euphorbia pulcherrima*)
NCS, S, 4'-10'

The beautiful Christmas plant should be pruned severely in the spring; then pruned again, lightly, in the early and the late summer. Keep night lights away for maximum flowering. Easier to grow than most think. Plant where it can be protected from frost.

28. **Powderpuff** (*Calliandra haematocephala*)
CS, S, 6'-12'

Large sprawling shrub with leaflet leaves and red, pink, or white flowers whose conspicuous stamens look like powderpuffs. Give lots of room and spray for thorn bugs.

29. **Rhaphiolepsis** (R. *indica*)   NC, S-Sh, 2'-4'

The India hawthorne is a sparse shrub with leathery leaves and clusters of fragrant, pinkish-white flowers (in late summer and fall). Not especially colorful, but popular in rich, seaside soils.

30. **Sasanqua** (*Camellia sasanqua*)
NC, S-Sh, 10'-15'

Fall reveals two-inch rosettes of rose, pink, or white flowers on this popular, north Florida, broadleaf evergreen.

31. **Saucer magnolia** (*Magnolia liliflora* 'Soulangeana')   N, S-Sh, 8'-12'

Freeform, unstructured shrub; deciduous; bears large, showy white flowers (with pink outside) in late winter before its leaves appear. Nice effect in Japanese garden.

32. **Shrimp plant** (*Beloperone guttata*)
NCS, S-Sh, 4'-6'

Curiosity shrub whose pinkish bracts droop over and look like shrimp throughout most of the warmer months. If frost-killed, cut it to the ground. It will return in the spring.

33. **Snow bush** (*Bregnia nivosa*)   CS, S, 6'-8'

Its dark red stems hold alternate, multicolored leaves speckled in red, pink, and white which provide year-round color in many landscapes in the warmer parts of the state. Likes sandy soils.

34. **Spanish bayonet** (*Yucca aloifolia*)
NCS, S-Sh, 5'-15'

Dangerously pointed, swordlike leaves make this a good barrier planting to keep out unwanted animals or as a cactus garden or rock garden specimen. Beautifully large clusters of brilliant white flowers dangle from panicles in spring. Y. *elephantipes* has soft leaves.

35. **Spirea** (*Spiraea* spp.)*   N, S-Sh, 4'-6'

Small-leafed, semi-weeping shrubs. In late winter, four-foot S. *thumbergii* produces hundreds of tiny white flowers along stems. Six-foot S. *vanhouttei* produces larger clusters in summer. Clay soils are preferred.

36. **Thryallis** (T. *glauca*)   NCS, S, 4'-8'

A fine-textured shrub with lots of small yellow flowers in colorful clusters. Grows throughout most of the year. Well-drained soils are best.

37. **Tibouchina** (T. *semidecandra*)   CS, S, 6'-12'

Large shrub with beautiful purple flower clusters that attract lots of attention. May be trained as a tree. Called princess flower. Prefers slightly acid soils. Protect from freeze.

38. **Turk's cap** (*Malvaviscus arboreus*) CS, S, 6'-10'

Looks like hibiscus whose dangling red flowers never fully open. Pink and white also available. More a curiosity plant than a showpiece.

The pale blue flowers of *Plumbago capensis* brighten any late summer landscape.

Refreshing springtime bloom of *spiraea* "Van Hoot."

Young cocoplum hedge (*Chrysobalanus icaco*).

Red leaf *Photinia glabra*, a glossy leaf hedge plant.

Split leaf philodendron (*P. selloum*) massed as foundation plant. Feathery *Asparagus sprengeri* front left.

SHRUBS FOR HEDGES AND ENCLOSURE SCREENS

NCS = planting zones
S-Sh = prefers sun or shade
6'-12' = heights commonly seen
* = photo

These shrubs are large in size and for the most part do not possess any particular coloring that would make them useful as specimen or accent plants. They should be planted along borders where enclosure is needed and behind shorter, more colorful shrubs or ground covers. Spacing between larger shrubs is often five feet or more.

1. **Arborvitae** (*Thuja orientalis*) NCS, S, 15'-30'
A needle evergreen with a dense, teardrop shape. Its needles are arranged vertically. Excellent for lining a circular drive on a large estate. Often seen overgrown on a small homesite. Spray for mites and juniper blight.

2. **Boxwood** (*Buxus microphylla*) NC, Sh, 3'-4'
Small-leafed or Japanese boxwood is often used in formal gardens where smaller, closely pruned hedges are desired. Likes fertile, nematode-free soils.

3. **Buttonwood, silver** (*Conocarpus erectus*)
S, S-Sh, 10'-30'
Buttonwood or buttonbush makes an excellent seaside barrier in south Florida where salt intrusion is common. Displays silver, downy leaves and tiny, reddish button cones. Grows to 50 feet if not trimmed. Tolerates alkaline soils.

4. **Cherry laurel** (*Prunus caroliniana*)
NC, S-Sh, 10'-30'
Tree most often kept pruned as a dense shrub, with glossy leaves of a reddish color when young. Foliage poisonous. Excellent for use as a hedge, especially when grown in fertile soils. Relative of the apple and pear.

5. **Cocculus** (*C. laurifolius*) NCS, S-Sh, 10'-20'
Shrub or pruned as small tree. May freeze to the ground. Attractive lance-shaped leaves (which droop) have three prominent veins.

6. **Cocoplum** (*Chrysobalanus icaco*)*
S, S-Sh, 3'-10'
Dense, symmetrical, evergreen leaves. Many varieties—beach, inland, miniature leaf. Its golf-ball-sized fruit is edible. Requires little attention. Handsome as a clipped hedge.

7. **Cuban laurel** (*Ficus retusa* 'Nitida')
CS, S-Sh, 10'-40'
In south Florida grows into a prized, clipped hedge. One of the strongest plants but is often freeze-killed in central Florida where it is grown as a large tree. Thrips can disfigure its leaves but are not a serious problem.

8. **Elaeagnus (E. *pungens*)**   NC, S-Sh, 10'-15'
A weeping, viny shrub easily sheared. Its leaves are silver underneath with numerous brown dots. An excellent choice where freeze hits hard. Called silverthorn because of its thorny canes.

9. **Eugenia (E. *paniculata*)**   S, S, 10'-20'
The Australian brush cherry of south Florida may be used as a hedge shrub or as a small tree, depending on its pruning. Its new growth is pink, turns to green and becomes dense, especially if sheared. Other cold-hardy Eugenias are available in north and central Florida.

10. **Fatsia (F. *japonica*)**   NCS, Sh, 3'-4'
For a short hedge, try fatsia. Its foot-wide leaves with deep clefts make an attractive display where horticultural interest is desired. Spray for sucking insects.

11. **Ficus benjamina (F. *benjamina*)**
      CS, S-Sh, 10'-40'
The weeping fig is much like Cuban laurel only lacier in its texture and more weeping. A cold-susceptible tree in central Florida but can be sheared successfully as dense hedge in Palm Beach and south Florida.

12. **Holly (*Ilex* spp.)***   NCS, S-Sh, 4'-20'
A number of hollies are available for hedge plantings. The medium-sized are I. *cornuta*, I. *rotunda*, I. *cassine*, and I. *vomitoria*,* and the shorter varieties are I. *crenata* and dwarf I. *vomitoria* (of north and central Florida). Some require male and female varieties to produce berries.

13. **Juniper (*Juniperus* spp.)***   NC, S, 2'-4'
Several junipers including the Pfitzer juniper, blue vase juniper, and the shorter andora juniper can grow into low hedges. These require no pruning and their feathery textures and off-green colors add much to the landscape.

14. **Ligustrum (*Ligustrum lucidum*)**
      NCS, S-Sh, 4'-20'
The green, glossy privet is one of central Florida's most popular hedges because of its easy care. Often pruned as small tree, its white flower clusters are not especially showy, but do provide a sweet, springtime fragrance.

15. **Osmanthus (O. *fragrens*)**   N, S-Sh, 5'-15'
Planted for its strong winter fragrance, osmanthus makes an excellent cold-hardy hedge and can be sheared to many heights. Its leaves are both smooth and prickly.

16. **Photinia (P. *glabra*)***   NC, S, 4'-8'
A long-time favorite of north Florida because of the reddish new growth. Now becoming a standard part of the central Florida landscape. Likes rich soils. Prune for compact hedge.

17. **Pittosporum (P. *tobira*)**   NCS, S-Sh, 4'-8'
In both green and variegated varieties, the "pitts" make splendid hedges requiring little shearing. Spray for Cercospora leaf spot and cottony cushion scale.

18. **Podocarpus (*Podocarpus* spp.)**
      NCS, S-Sh, 5'-15'
P. *gracilior* is a dense feathery species of south Florida, while P. *macrophylla* is a dense, less feathery species which grows statewide and will actually reach 40 or 50 feet if not kept pruned. A handsome tree, but almost always sheared as a barrier, especially to produce a formal hedge. Avoid planting in low sites where water is trapped.

19. **Selloum (*Philodendron selloum*)***
      CS, S-Sh, 5'-10'
Its huge leaves growing from the ground make any landscape a tropical scene. A dense, herbaceous perennial. Likes fertilizer and water.

20. **Viburnum (*Viburnum* spp.)***
      NCS, S-Sh, 4'-10'
Several species are used, including the fragrant, glossy-leafed V. *odoratissimum* and the shorter, leathery-leafed V. *suspensum*. Leaf spot and nematodes may be a problem.

21. **Wax myrtle (*Myrica cerifera*)***
      NCS, S-Sh, 10'-20'
A small, multitrunk tree or shrub (depending on its pruning) seen growing in the wilds of Florida. Holds its leaves in south Florida. Inexpensive but is somewhat brittle and short-lived.

Wax myrtle (*Myrica cerifera*) emerges from a bed of dwarf Chinese holly (*Ilex Cornuta*) while *Viburnum odoratissimum* hides airconditioning unit. Feathery tree at rear is Australian pine (*Casuarina equisetifolia*).

SHRUBS WITH SHOWY FRUIT

NCS = planting zone
S-Sh = prefers sun or shade
6'-12' = heights commonly seen
* = photo)

In Florida many plants arouse curiosity or exhibit beauty through their fruits or berries. Here are several prized by landscapers. Most are not particularly edible.

1. **Beauty berry** (*Callicarpa americana*)
NC, Sh, 4'-6'
Bare in winter, this coarse-textured native shrub bears lilac flowers in spring followed by purple clusters of small berries. Great for woodland settings.

2. **Carissa** (*Carissa grandiflora*)   CS, S, 4'-8'
The evergreen Natal plum is popular as a foundation shrub where its white pinwheel flowers are followed by golfball-sized red fruit popular in jellies. Salt-tolerant and available in dwarf forms.

3. **Coral ardesia** (*Ardesia crenata*) NC, Sh, 3'-5'
Attractive clusters of coral-red berries hang from leggy branches in cooler months. Called Christmas berry. Likes acidic, rich, nematode-free soil.

4. **Golden dewdrop** (*Duranta repens*)
CS, S, 6'-12'
Poisonous yellow berries hang on drooping stems after tiny blue flowers appear in warm months. Needs space to spread.

5. **Holly** (*Ilex* spp.)   NC, S-Sh, 4'-10'
A number of shrub species available with smooth or prickly leaves and red or black berries. Most prefer an acid, fertile soil. Purchase them when fruit is showing.

6. **Jasmine, orange** (*Murraya paniculata*)
CS, S-Sh, 6'-12'
Fragrant flower clusters like that of an orange tree produce clumps of colorful, pointed, red berries in warmer months. Can be used as small tree, hedge, or foundation plant. Guard against nematodes.

7. **Lime berry** (*Triphasia trifolia*) S, S-Sh, 4'-6'
Similar to Severinia but with red berries. Excellent for low hedge or foundation plant. Protect against nematodes.

8. **Malpighia** (*M. coccigera*)   S, Sh, 1'-2'
Dwarf, very prickly holly shrub has attractive red berries most of the year. Use in sweeping borders when backed by taller shrubs of contrasting colors. Rich, nematode-free soil is best.

9. **Nandina** (*N. domestica*)   NC, S-Sh, 5'-7'
Reedlike unbranching stems bear feathery leaves that turn red in the fall as bright red berries begin to appear. Likes superior soils. Also known as heavenly bamboo.

Sea grape (*Coccoloba uvifera*) trained as a hedge.

10. **Pyracantha** (*P. coccinea*)   NC, S-Sh, 8'-16'
Also known as firethorn, this shrub has thorny branches bearing showy red or orange berries in the fall. Popular as espalier plant but needs frequent pruning. Spray for mites on leaves.

11. **Sea grape** (*Coccoloba uvifera*)* CS, S, 10'-20'
Highly salt-tolerant shrub that needs lots of room. The huge round leaves are bronze when young, then red just before they fall. Purple grapes hang during warmer months and are used in jellies.

12. **Severinia boxthorn** (*S. buxifolia*)
CS, S-Sh, 4'-6'
A dwarf, compact shrub useful where a sure traffic stopper is needed. Thorny branches hold shiny, black berries. Protect from hard freeze.

TREES WITH SHOWY COLOR

NCS = planting zones
S-Sh = prefers sun or shade
10'-20' = heights commonly seen
* = photo

Flowering trees are highly prized in Florida because we have such a long blooming season, and because we can plant the most colorful species of the Caribbean as well as favorites of the southern U.S. Some listed here show their beauty through their leaves. Plant several freely as accents and to provide year-round interest.

1. African tulip tree (*Spathodea campanulata*)
S, S, 20'-40'
Late winter flowers of reddish-orange peer through compound, evergreen leaves. This is a good choice for an avenue tree or for shading a patio.

2. American holly (*Ilex opaca*) NC, S-Sh, 20'-30'
Several prickly leafed varieties including 'Savannah,' 'Howard,' 'Dupré,' and a smoother leafed 'East Palatka.' Most American hollies have red berries and look best when pruned in a pyramid shape with foliage beginning low near the ground.

3. Bombax (*B. malabaricum*) S, S, 40'-60'
Bold red tulip-shaped flowers appear on bare branches midwinter. Thorny, buttressed trunk has horizontal branches. Admired for its mid-winter offering of color. Cousin to the kapok tree (*Ceiba pentandra*)* whose pinkish-white flowers are not as showy but whose huge buttresses at the base of the trunk are a curiosity when given plenty of room.

4. Bottlebrush, weeping (*Callistemon citrinus*)
CS, S, 10'-15'
Early spring produces red, dangling bottlebrush flowers on weeping branches to announce the end of summer. Use where a feathery textured, short tree is desired.

5. Chaste tree (*Vitex agnus-castus*)
NCS, S-Sh, 10'-15'
Leafless in winter, gray-green leaves and terminal spikes of lilac or white flowers appear in midsummer. Use near a patio where the fragrant flowers can be appreciated from this small tree.

6. Coral tree (*Erythrina crista-gallii*)
CS, S-Sh, 15'-20'
Tiny thorns line the stems. Bright red flowers begin appearing in late summer followed by long brown seed pods.

7. Crape myrtle (*Lagerstroemia indica*)
NCS, S, 10'-15'
For a short tree full of colorful clusters of white, pink, purple, or red flowers in summer, this one is hard to beat. South Florida grows the profusely flowered queen crape myrtle (L. *speciosa*) whose pink or purple blossoms cause limbs to sag.

Cassia fistula, the golden shower tree, on a Naples street corner.

Colorful white bracts of dogwood (*Cornus florida*) brighten a Gainesville street.

8. Dogwood (*Cornus florida*)*   NC, S-Sh, 15'-25'
In cooler regions, spring is heralded by the bold white bracts appearing on bare limbs. Autumn brings red berries and reddish leaves before they fall. Pink dogwoods do not grow successfully in Florida as it is not cold enough.

9. Fringe tree (*Chionanthus virginia*)
NC, S-Sh, 20'-25'
Bare spring limbs produce loose clusters of tiny white flowers as leaves appear Dark berries dangle in late summer. Likes moisture.

10. Geiger tree (*Cordia sebania*)S, S-Sh, 20'-25'
Large evergreen leaves and showy scarlet flowers that resemble a loose geranium in summer make this seaside tree popular.

11. Goldenrain (*Koelreuteria formosana*)
NC, S, 20'-30'
A tree for all seasons. Spring brings a flush of light green leaves to the bare winter branches. Summer offers tall panicles of yellow flowers followed by pink papery capsules—a favorite of the fall landscape. Easy to maintain.

12. Golden shower (*Cassia fistula*)*
S, S-sh, 20'-30'
Large, even, compound leaves held year-round with golden yellow flower spikes appearing in summer followed by narrow brown pods dangling some two feet long. Cassia is a large, colorful genus.

13. Jacaranda (*Jacaranda acutifolia*) CS, S, 30'-40'
Large umbrella tree with lacy double compound leaves that drop in winter. Huge clusters of blue-purple flowers are quite showy in late spring, which then cover the ground like blue snow.

14. Lignum vitae (*Guaiacum officinale*)
S, S-Sh, 15'-20'
Twisted trunk bears dense, feathery, compound leaves year-round and attractive, pale blue flowers in summer followed by small, yellow, heart-shaped capsules. Use near a patio or where a small tree is desired.

15. Mimosa (*Albizia julibrissin*)   NC, S, 20'-30'
A lacy, deciduous, umbrella tree whose delicate, pink pom-poms look especially good in a Japanese garden but are used anywhere a summer canopy is desired.

16. Orchid tree (*Bauhinia* spp.)
CS, S-Sh, 15'-20'
Large, goat-foot-shaped leaves fall in winter in central Florida when a splendid display of orchid flowers appears in shades of white, red, or purple to brighten the landscape. South Florida blooming season is longer (depending on variety) and leaves may remain. The Hong Kong orchid tree is prized in south Florida for its larger flowers.

17. Pongam (*Pongamia pinnata*) S, S-Sh, 30'-40'
The large, compound leaves are held year-round. Pinkish white flowers in clusters typical of the pea family appear in spring. Strong tree good for wind break or avenue planting.

18. Redbud (*Cercis canadensis*) NC, S-Sh, 20'-30'
Hundreds of tiny, pink flowers grace dark, bare limbs in late winter before large, heart-shaped leaves appear. Popular in north Florida where it grows best in fertile, acid soils containing plenty of organic matter.

19. Red maple (*Acer rubrum*) NC, S-Sh, 40'-60'
Since this is ia swamp tree give it plenty of water. Its leaves often turn yellow to red before they fall. In late winter tiny red flowers flush out, followed by scarlet, winged seed pods that make a splendid color display. Tip borers are not a serious threat; they prune the tree.

20. Royal poinciana (*Delonix regia*) S, S, 25'-35'
Magnificent red summertime flowers blaze atop this dense, feathery umbrella tree, which inspired the famous "Song of the Trees." Called the "flamboyant" in the Caribbean. Perhaps the most colorful tree in the world. Won't take freeze.

21. Shaving brush tree (*Pachira* spp.)
S, S-Sh, 20'-30'
Red shaving brush flowers appear on bare limbs in late winter to announce the coming spring. Most striking when grown in rich, moist locations.

22. Star magnolia (*Magnolia stellata*)
N, S-Sh, 10'-20'
Large shrub or small tree depending upon pruning. Attractive, white, starlike flowers appear on bare branches before soft leaves appear in spring. Prefers fertile, acid soils that are well drained.

23. Tabebuia (*Tabebuia* spp.)   S, S-Sh, 15'-30'
About 50 species available. Perhaps the most popular is T. *argentia*, the tree of gold or silver trumpet tree that displays giant clusters of bold yellow flowers in spring before silvery leaves appear. T. *pallida* has less showy, purple flowers. Excellent patio trees.

Hedge-trained Australian pine (*Casuarina equisetifolia*).

Leaves and trunk of box elder (*Acer negundo*).

TREES FOR SHADE OR WIND BREAK

NCS = planting zones
S-Sh = prefers sun or shade
10'-20' = heights commonly seen
* = photo

The following trees are selected because of their strength to block out wind along a barrier or their ability to provide shade. Some are deciduous and most are not grown for color. Be careful about planting large, vigorous trees near walks or foundations where they are likely to crack concrete.

1. **Acacia, earleaf** (*Acacia auriculaeformis*)
   S, S-Sh, 15'-25'
   This fast grower tends to be brittle but grows in the poorest of soils. Broadleaf evergreen with loose, upright growth. Yellow flower cluster not very showy.

2. **Almond** (*Terminalia catappa*)   S, S, 20'-30'
   Tropical almond has huge leaves in a tiered, symmetrical head. Superb for wind and salt resistance. Leaves turn red before they fall.

3. **Australian pine** (*Casuarina equisetifolia*)*
   CS, S-Sh, 40'-50'
   Highly salt-tolerant and often used as a wind break along the seashore. Feathery upright head. Not a real pine. Also pruned as a hedge. Seedlings collected in the wild often produce unsightly "suckers" in your lawn. Purchase only cultivated plants found in nurseries.

4. **Black olive** (*Bucida buceras*) S, S-Sh, 25'-35'
   Common avenue tree of south Florida because of dense, symmetrical, evergreen head. Good wind and salt tolerance.

5. **Box elder** (*Acer negundo*)*   N, S-Sh, 30'-50'
   A type of maple, deciduous, hardy, drought-resistant, and fast-growing.

6. **Brazilian pepper** (*Schinus terebinthifolius*)
   CS, S, 15'-20'
   Called Florida holly because of the bright red Christmas berries. Umbrella head becomes huge if not pruned. Grows fast and needs lots of room. Not a good avenue tree, too wild. Outlawed in some communities as a fast-spreading exotic that overtakes native plants. Very hard to get rid of once established.

7. **Camphor** (*Cinnamomum camphora*)*
   NCS, S-Sh, 30'-40'
   A handsome, symmetrical, broadleaf evergreen that grows throughout the state. Slow but sturdy, casting dense shade. Low branching for picturesque effect.

8. **Carrotwood** (*Cupania anacardioidres*)
   CS, S-Sh, 25'-35'
   Excellent choice, evergreen leaves, no particular pest problem, tolerates wind and salt spray, medium grower, twisting branches for character, but subject to freeze.

9. Cedar, Deodar (*Cedrus deodara*)

NCS, S, 20'-40'

Handsome, silvery, Christmas tree evergreen with bluish tint.

10. Cedar, southern red (*Juniper silicicola*)

NCS, S-Sh, 20'-30'

Columnar if pruned as a shrub, but the large pyramidal head makes as good a barrier as a tall tree. Easily transplanted from seedling. Needle evergreen.

11. Chinese tallow (*Sapium sebiferum*)

NC, S-Sh, 20'-30'

Deciduous, fast grower with dancing leaves. As wide as it is tall. Prefers soils slightly acidic.

12. Cuban laurel (*Ficus retusa* 'Nitida')*

CS, S-Sh, 30'-40'

Used as a hedge or a tree. As a tree it is massive, fast growing, sturdy and dense, but surface roots may hinder lawn mowing. May freeze in central Florida.

13. Cypress, bald (*Taxodium distichum*)

NCS, S-Sh, 40'-60'

Loves water, so excellent choice along lake bank—even a few feet in the water. But thrives in dry soil also. Stepping stone slices from lower trunk and ''knees'' are sold along Florida roadsides. Slow grower.

14. Dalbergia (*D. sissoo*)   CS, S-Sh, 30'-40'

The India rosewood has deciduous, round, pointed leaves in a loose, symmetrical head. Grows fast and has no significant pests.

15. Ear Tree (*Enterolobium cyclocarpum*)

CS, S-Sh, 50'-60'

Huge, spreading head has feathery, compound, deciduous leaves. Grows fast, a bit brittle, and surface roots tend to interfere where there is lawn below. Brown pods resemble ears.

16. Elm, Dwarf (*Ulmus pumila*)   NC, S, 15'-25'

Handsome, symmetrical, small tree with deciduous leaves and fast growth. Larger species available with loose, delicate-looking heads.

17. Eucalyptus (*Eucalyptus* spp.) CS, S, 40'-50'

Perhaps the fastest grower of Florida shade trees, as much as 15 feet a season. Grows easily in sand or clay, wet or dry. A little messy, evergreen, and somewhat brittle. No pests.

18. Gumbo-limbo (*Bursera simaruba*)

S, S-Sh, 40'-50'

Curious, oily, brown, peeling bark. Deciduous and fast grower yet a sturdy wind break. Unique, popular species.

19. Harpulia (*H. arborea*)   S, S-Sh, 40'-50'

Dense shade cast from a thick head. Red, double seed pods which are not very showy but interesting. Used as an avenue tree in Miami.

Camphor tree (*Cinnamonum camphora*)

Cuban laurel (*Ficus retusa*) hedge behind a closely cropped row of Australian pine (*Casuarine equisetifolia*). Avenue palms are coconut.

Mature live oak (*Quercus virginiana*) in typical Florida jungle setting of vines, moss, and tree fern.

Young live oak (*Quercus virginiana*) surrounded by *Pittosporum tobira* and *Ilex vomitoria* pruned into balls.

Ficus elastica 'Decora,' the rubber tree of south Florida.

20. **Magnolia** (M. *grandiflora*)   NC, S, 40'-60'
Pyramidal, dense, with large, glossy, evergreen leaves, the magnolia is a favorite of the old South. Large, white, waxy, springtime flowers are spectacular when cut for indoor show. Not usually considered with flowering trees.

21. **Mahogany** (*Swietenia mahogani*)
   S, S-Sh, 25'-35'
Salt-tolerant, deciduous compound foliage. Brown, softball-sized pods dangle in cooler months. Sturdy shade tree.

22. **Oak** (*Quercus* spp.)*   NCS, S-Sh, 30'-50'
The laurel oak (Q. *laurifolia*) is deciduous with superior symmetry. The live oak (Q. *virginiana*) is evergreen with twisting, picturesque boughs. Both are strong, medium-fast growers. The live oak resists salt.

23. **Pine** (*Pinus* spp.)   NCS, S-Sh, 40'-60'
Use where broken shade is desired for growing azaleas and other plants that like filtered sunlight. Slash pine (P. *elliotii*) does well in moist locations, sand pine (P. *clausa*) in dry. Both salt-tolerant. Count on dealing with fallen needles and cones.

24. **Punk tree** (*Melaleuca leucadendra*)
   CS, S, 30'-40'
Narrow, thin tree of sparse top and exceptionally attractive, white, soft, multilayered bark. Unpopular today because of common allergies to the mashed-potato-scented, bottlebrush flowers. Very salt-tolerant.

25. **Rubber tree*** (*Ficus elastica*) S, S-Sh, 20'-40'
Huge, dense, umbrella crown is characteristic of this large-leafed member of the fig family. Fast grower needs lots of room. Cuttings sold as house plants.

26. **Sapodilla** (*Achras zapota*)   S, S, 20'-30'
Smaller, symmetrical tree with evergreen leaves on whorling branches. Salt-tolerant and sturdy, it is a popular lawn and avenue tree.

27. **Satan leaf** (*Chrysophyllum oliviforma*)
   S, Sh, 20'-25'
Huge, textured, evergreen leaves with copper undersides on this small tree. Best under a canopy of taller trees.

28. **Sausage tree** (*Kigelia pinnate*)* S, S, 20'-30'
Giant bologna-shaped pods nearly two feet long hang curiously from compound, deciduous leaves. Hand pollinate night-blooming flowers in case bats don't. An eye-stopper.

29. **Sea grape** (*Coccoloba uvifera*)   CS, S, 15'-20'
Prune this highly salt-tolerant shrub into a tree shape. Giant, red-veined, round leaves held year-round. Sprawling. Also makes a good hedge.

30. **Silk oak** (*Grevillea robusta*)   CS, S, 40'-60'
Pyramidal with grayish feathery leaves in pyramidal shape. Fast grower. Needs room. Messy when spring bloom falls.

31. **Sweet gum** (*Liquidamber styraciflua*)
NCS, S-Sh, 50'-60'
Easy, fast shade. Star-shaped leaves show fall color. The gumball fruits and winged twigs are popular as Christmas cuttings.

32. **Sycamore** (*Platinus occidentalis*)
NCS, S-Sh, 50'-60'
Three-lobed leaves drop in the fall from this fast grower. Sheds its attractive bark in the winter. Tolerates a variety of soils.

33. **Tamarind, wild** (*Lysiloma bahamensis*)*
S, S-Sh, 30'-50'
Tiny leaflets give a feathery, tropical appearance to this mildly salt-tolerant shade tree. Bare in winter, tiny clusters of greenish-white flowers in April. Abundant in Biscayne Bay area and Key West. Young seedlings may be dug and transplanted from the wild.

34. **Tulip tree** (*Liriodendron tulipifera*)
NC, S-Sh, 60'-80'
Very large tree with good symmetry. Deciduous, pyramidal, and fast. Prefers moist soils but thrives on any.

35. **Wax myrtle** (*Myrica cerifera*)
NCS, S-Sh, 15'-25'
Small native with picturesque shape. Good windbreak near salt water. Open branching near maturity. Not long-lived like hardwoods.

36. **Weeping fig** (*Ficus benjamina*)*
CS, S-Sh, 20'-40'
Handsome, symmetrical, dense. If not pruned as hedge grows quickly to weeping shade tree. May need protection in central Florida. Excellent avenue tree.

37. **White birch** (*Betula* spp.)   N, S, 30'-60'
Several birches grow in the cooler regions. Deciduous, hardy, most have flaking, whitish bark and thrive in moist to normal soils. Yellow, river, paper, and gray birch (often in clumps) are common species.

38. **Willow** (*Salix babylonica*)   NC, S, 20'-35'
Long, weeping branches are a favorite. Likes lots of water, such as along a ditchbank or pond. Large head grows rapidly. Usually deciduous.

Sausage tree (*Kigelia pinnata*).

Wild tamarind (*Lysiloma behamensis*) dangles its lacy foliage along famed Duval Street in Key West.

Weeping willow (*Salix babylonica*) prefers wet soil.

Areca, cane, or bamboo palm (*Chrysalidocarpus lutescens*) as it grows in south Florida.

State tree, cabbage palm (*Sabal palmetto*).

PALMS

NCS = planting zone
S-Sh = prefers sun or shade
30'-40' = heights commonly seen
* = photo

To many people Florida means palm trees. Florida palms display either long, *pinnate* leaves that sway lazily in the breeze, or fanlike, *palmate* leaves whose dried, older fronds clatter in the wind. They possess either single or multiple trunks. Some clump palms are pruned to a single trunk but new growths must be constantly pruned off as they emerge from the ground. If you need a single trunk specimen it is better to choose one to begin with. Multiple-clump palms show best when trunks are kept to an odd number such as five, seven, or nine. Designers like to see a clump of foliage at ground level, several trunks emerging through the foliage mass, topped by another cluster of fronds at the top. Closely related to the grass family (monocots), palms have a short, shallow, dense root system making them easy to transplant.

1. Areca palm (*Chrysalidocarpus lutescens*)*
   CS, S-Sh, 15'-25'
   This is a clump palm also called Madagascar, cane, bamboo, and yellow palm because its fronds tend to have yellow stems. In central Florida a potted specimen or dense, feathery backdrop. In Naples they are grown as tall, multi-trunk specimens on front lawns. Tolerates salt and likes rich, acid soils.

2. Cabbage palm (*Sabal palmetto*)*
   NCS, S-Sh, 30'-60'
   Our state tree seen everywhere in the wild, salt-tolerant, and used any way imaginable. Single trunk, palmate fronds. Indians and pioneers ate the cabbage-tasting hearts from young trees. Mature trees may be ordered from landscape nurseries who dig them from the wild. Plant deep and water heavily the first season.

3. Canary Island date palm (*Phoenix canariensis*)*
   NCS, S, 20'-40'
   Called pineapple palm when young due to its pineapple appearance. With thick, single trunk and stiff pinnate fronds, this majestic palm needs plenty of room. The orange dates are not edible. The lower base of the fronds is thorny.

4. Chamaedorea (*Chamaedorea* spp.)
   CS, Sh, 8'-12'
   A dwarf cluster palm for shaded patios or urns. Some species are single-trunked. Often used as bamboo without the risk of the rapid spreading common with bamboo.

5. **Chinese fan palm** (*Livistonia chinensis*)
CS, S-Sh, 15'-28'
Single trunk with large, handsome fronds, the bases of which have sharp thorns that curve inward. Tips of older fronds weep. A beautiful fan palm.

6. **Coconut** (*Cocos nucifera*)*　　S, S, 30'-50'
Highly salt-tolerant with picturesque trunk that bends and enlarges where it approaches the ground. Stiff pinnate fronds. Select newer varieties that are resistant to the disease called lethal yellows. The fruit is edible.

7. **Cocos australis** (*Butia capitata*)
NCS, S, 10'-20'
Previously misnamed, the pindo palm is a favorite as far north as South Carolina because of its C-shaped, bluish, pinnate leaves. Needs plenty of room since its fronds are low to the ground.

8. **Cocos plumosa** (*Syagrus romanzoffianum*)
CS, S, 20'-30'
Relatively inexpensive with long, soft, pinnate fronds that dance in the gentlest breeze. Often planted in pairs slanted outward to give a clump effect. Colorful, white flowers followed by orange dates (nonedible) which are sometimes messy and attract bees. Previously classified as genus *Arecastrum*.

9. **European fan palm** (*Chamaerops humilii*)
NCS, S-Sh, 9'-10'
Hardy, stiff fans of grayish tint that grow upon short trunks, single or clump. Good where space is limited.

10. **Fishtail palm** (*Caryota mitis*) S, S-Sh, 15'-20'
A clump palm whose pinnate fronds have wide, fishtail-shaped leaflets. Commonly used as potted specimens where shade is intense. Like most palms, prefers fertile, well-drained soils but survives in almost all soils.

11. **Lady palm** (*Rhapis excellsa*)　　NCS, Sh, 4'-8'
Small clump of dense, palmate fronds whose fingers are widely parted. Sometimes cleaned out to reveal tiny trunks. Expensive, in demand, great for urns, likes shade and moist soil.

12. **MacArthur palm** (*Ptychosperma macarthurii*)
S, S-Sh, 15'-20'
Cluster palm with thin trunks, dense growth, pinnate fronds whose leaflets appear beaten off at the tips. Needs space but useful where a small clump palm is desired.

See why *Phoenix canariensis* is called pineapple palm?

Salt-tolerant coconut palms (*Cocos nucifera*) line ritzy Fifth Avenue in Naples near the Gulf.

Multitrunk *Paurotis wrightii* shows new trunks emerging at ground level.

Mature king sago palms (*Cycas revoluta*) emerge through a dense bed of variegated *Pittosporum tobira*.

13. **Paurotis palm** (*Paurotis wrightii*)*
CS, S-Sh, 15'-25'
Popular clump palm with fan leaves. Excellent choice for residential use as accents or on corners because of slender trunks. Called Cape Sable palm and has good salt tolerance.

14. **Phoenix reclinata** (*P. reclinata*)
NCS, S-Sh, 20'-30'
Reclining trunks from a single cluster bear stiff, pinnate leaves with murderous thorns near the base. Popular and expensive but highly majestic when pruned with foliage clusters at top and bottom with clean trunks showing through the middle.

15. **Pygmy date palm** (*Phoenix roebelenii*)
CS, S-Sh, 4'-8'
Newer varieties remain low to the ground. A good, short accent. Soft, shiny pinnate leaves gracefully curve but hold sharp thorns near the base. Common in urns also. Slow growing.

16. **Royal palm** (*Roystonea regia*) S, S-Sh, 40'-60'
Most stately single-trunk species. Emerald green upper trunk with long, graceful fronds. This is a formal avenue palm as seen in Palm Beach and Sarasota. Likes abundant moisture. R. *elata*, a Florida native planted at the Hialeah race course, is not as popular.

17. **Sago, king** (*Cycas revoluta*)* NCS, S-Sh, 4'-8'
Stiff, short fronds on this small plant, which is popular as a low, accent palm. A prevalent virus makes fronds occasionally appear yellow and twisted. Comes in male and female.

18. **Sago, queen** (*Cycas circinalis*)
CS, S-Sh, 10'-20'
Soft, flat, long fronds shiny on top, droop gracefully. Thick, single trunk. Graceful, free-standing specimen needs plenty of room since fronds are often low to the ground.

19. **Solitaire palm** (*Ptychosperma elegans*)
S, S-Sh, 15'-20'
Called seaforthia by some growers. A good choice for urns or where space is limited. Thin, single trunk with rings on lower portion. Pinnate fronds with showy red fruits in summer.

20. **Travelers palm** (*Ravenala madagascariensis*)
CS, S-Sh, 10'-20'
Huge, bananalike leaves form a giant, symmetrical fan. Leaves solid until split by wind. Appears very tropical and needs protection from cold. Not actually a palm.

21. **Washington palm** (*Washingtonia robusta*)
NCS, S-Sh, 40'-60'
Huge and handsome fan fronds when young but not popular on home grounds due to its tall, single trunk. Plant around tall, municipal buildings or along avenues.

VINES

NCS = planting zone
S-Sh = prefers sun or shade
* = photo

A broad selection of vines, both evergreen and flowering, are available to the Florida landscaper. Many species have clinging tendrils that support themselves like the *Ficus pumila* on the "halls of ivy" at the University of Florida in Gainesville. Others are not so adapted and must be tied to a wall or trellis. Some are allowed to creep over the ground and make excellent ground covers (see ground cover list). Many, such as bougainvillea and certain jasmines, may be grown as shrubs if kept pruned. Careful selection can produce a continuation of bloom throughout the year, but several of these bloomers are deciduous.

1. Allamanda (A. *cathartica*)   CS, S
Poisonous but beautiful with bold, yellow trumpet flowers. Shiny evergreen leaves in long whorls need protection from freeze. Long blooming season during warm months. May be trained as a shrub. Needs support as a vine.

2. Bougainvillea (*Bougainvillea spp.*)   CS, S
Brilliant colored bracts of red, orange, magenta, and white make this Florida's most popular vine in early spring. Huge walls of bougainvillea are grown at St. Petersburg's famed Sunken Gardens. Thorny, woody stems need tying. Allow plenty of room. Acid soil is preferred.

3. Carolina jasmine (*Gelsemium sempervirens*)*
NC, S-Sh
Yellow jasmine, or jessamine, twists its reddish stems around supports and displays bright yellow, fragrant trumpet flowers in late winter. Not rampant. Likes moisture.

4. Cat's claw (*Doxanthus unquis-cati*)*
NCS, S-Sh
Rampant and dense, this tiny vine clings tenaciously and covers rapidly. Attractive yellow trumpet flowers appear in spring.

5. Chalice vine (*Solandra guttata*)   CS, Sh
Tender, rampant grower producing white to gold cup-shaped flowers nearly a foot long in summer. Has tenacious roots and requires a strong trellis to support its heavy weight. Yields tropical appearance.

6. Combratum (C. *grandiflorum*)   S, S
Summer months bring out giant, red, toothbrush-looking flowers on rampant vines that twine. Evergreen leaves to six inches and slender. Use to cover a large fence.

7. Coral vine (*Antigonon leptopus*)   NCS, S
Tendril clinging, herbaceous stems hold heart-shaped leaves and rows of small pink or white flowers in late summer and fall. Often killed to ground in colder regions, so don't use at the front of the home.

Carolina yellow jessamine vine (*Gelsemium sempervirens*).

8. Creeping fig (*Ficus pumila*)*   NCS, S-Sh
A small-leafed, clinging species in the famous banyan or rubber plant family. Contains milky sap, no flowers, dense evergreen. Tiny leaves triple in size when grown upward several feet. Vigorous grower in any soil.

9. Flame vine, Florida (*Pyrostegia ignea*)
CS, S-Sh
Evergreen and rampant vine with tendrils. Late winter brings out the showy, orange clusters of tubular blossoms whose five tips curl back. Quickly covers large trellis or chainlink fence.

10. Herald's trumpet (*Beaumontia grandiflora*)
CS, S-Sh
Displays giant, eight-inch trumpet flowers, white with pink tips and green veins in summer. Very fragrant. Dense growth requires strong support. Frost kills it back.

Cat's claw (*Doxanthus unquis-cati*) clings to wall.

11. Jasmine (*Jasminum* spp.) CS, S

Many species available. Commonly planted are the popular Confederate jasmine (*Trachelospermum jasminoides*), the shining jasmine (*J. nitidum*) with feathery clusters of fragrant flowers, and downy or star jasmine (*J. multiflorum*) with starlike, nonfragrant flowers. Each has small but numerous white flowers. Sprawling vines are often trained as a shrub. Primrose jasmine (*J. mesnyi*) has small yellow flowers in late winter and survives north Florida's cooler winters.

12. Mexican flame vine (*Senecio confusus*) CS, S-Sh

Easy-to-grow evergreen that quickly covers a tall fence or the side of a building if tied in place. Profusion of orange, daisylike flowers borne in warm months. Frost usually kills it to the ground but it returns.

13. Painted trumpet (*Clytostoma callistegiodes*) NCS, S-Sh

Attractive trumpet flowers up to three inches long display their lavender hue in springtime followed by four-inch seed capsules. Evergreen leaves and tendrils on rampant vines.

14. Pandorea (*Podranea ricasoliana*) CS, S-Sh

A sprawling vine with delicate, bell-shaped flowers, pink with a red throat. Evergreen, compound leaves and foot-long seed pods that follow the spring bloom. Needs support and nematode-free soils.

15. Philodendron (*Philodendron* spp.)* CS, S-Sh

There are a vast number of vining philodendrons which display huge, shiny leaves of interesting shapes. All of them cling and produce no flowers. Many are tender to frost. They are often sold as house plants or in hanging baskets. Philodendrons are best grown up the trunks of pines or oaks and prefer organic, acidic, fertile, well-drained soils.

16. Pothos (*Scindapsis* spp.)* CS, S-Sh

This common house plant with variegated, heart-shaped leaves develops giant, attractive foliage when grown upright on a tree trunk. Plant several at the base of a tree for year-round attraction. Clings by itself. Used as a ground cover where it has plenty of room and protection from frost.

17. Queen's wreath (*Petrea volubilis*) S, S-Sh

Foot-long clusters of wisterialike flowers are purple against the side of a house in early summer. Leaves very rough to touch. Moderate fertility in well-drained soils.

18. Rangoon creeper (*Quisqualis indica*) S, S-Sh

This one loses its leaves in winter. New leaves are brownish. Small pinwheel flowers begin white then turn red in warm months. Let it sprawl over a fence.

19. Syngonium (*Syngonium* spp.) CS, Sh

Similar to split-leaf philodendron, the many species develop huge, lancelike, shiny foliage. Plant at the base of palms where it will climb and cling for a real jungle effect. Prefers organic, acid soils.

20. Tecomaria (*Tecomaria capensis*) CS, S

The cape honeysuckle or tecoma has evergreen, compound leaves and small, trumpet flowers that hang in orange clusters during warm months. Easily trained as a shrub or small tree. Needs support as a vine. Little attention.

21. Wisteria (*Wisteria sinensis*) NC, Sh

Another deciduous vine with compound leaves. Purple or white, pea-pod clusters dangle in spring. Popular in the old South for covering arbors. Easy to grow. Rarely seen in central Florida.

22. Wooley congea (*Congea tomentosa*) S, S

A sprawler with fuzzy leaves and clusters of tiny flowers that change from white to lavender to purple to gray in early spring. Needs strong support and may be trained as a shrub.

Variety of cropped hedges mark the entrance to this garden. Creeping fig (*Ficus pumila*) clings to the wall.

Double-Role Ground Cover

On the ground, pothos (*Scindapsis* spp.) spreads quickly to make an attractive ground cover. As a vine clinging to tree trunks its leaves grow over two feet long.

Screw pine (*Pandanus utilis*).

Dracaena marginata stock plant makes a handsome, multitrunk house plant.

This Norfolk Island pine (*Araucaria excelsa*) produced a triple trunk after leader was damaged.

ACCENT PLANTS

NCS = planting zone
S-Sh = prefers sun or shade
6'-10' = heights commonly seen
* = photo

In the midst of a plant bed massed with flowers or ground covers it is desirable to plant a *single* specimen for accent. Such plants range in height from four feet to the size of a small tree and possess enough color or interesting shape to stand alone as a focal point. Accent plants are also used at the corners of the home, at the end of a hedge, or framing an entry drive. Many are planted in large tubs or urns for the patio. Accent plants may be shrubs, small trees or even tall perennials. It all depends on how they are used in the landscape. Following are several excellent choices for accent plants.

1. **Aralia** (*Polyscias balfouriana*) S, S-Sh, 10'-20'
This is often used as a hedge but it makes a handsome accent plant when pruned as a small tree. Broad evergreen leaves with variegated markings and serrated margins.

2. **Bamboo** (**Numerous genera**)   NCS, S-Sh
A number of bamboo make good accent plants but be careful to choose the smaller varieties that don't grow tall or spread rampantly. Try switchcans (*Arundinaria tecta*) or *Chamaedorea* spp.

3. **Bird of paradise** (*Strelitzia reginae*)
CS, Sh, 4'
Where a small accent is needed try this tropical clump of swordlike leaves that displays a spectacle of bird-looking flowers in orange and blue. *Strelitzia nicolai* is a 20-foot species. Fertile, moist, acid soils are best.

4. **Cedar, southern red** (*Juniperus silicicola*)
NCS, S-Sh, 10'-20'
Pruned as a columnar evergreen or taller Christmas tree shape, cedar is easy to maintain in moderately fertile soil. Withstands considerable salt air and salty soil. Good choice for beach property.

5. **Cedar, Deodar** (*Cedrus deodara*)
NCS, S, 20'-40'
A blue-green Christmas tree that greatly resembles the northern spruce. Keep pruned into compact, formal shape. Nice for color variation in evergreen bed.

6. **Dracena** (*Dracaena* spp.)*   CS, Sh, 5'-10'
Many species with variegated, swordlike leaves atop thumb-size woody trunks loosely resemble miniature palms. Likes rich, moist soils.

7. **Elephant ear**   NCS, S-Sh, 4'-8'
Numerous genera and species are called elephant ear. Their huge, triangular leaves emerging from root clusters make a handsome, tropical addition. Popular also as urn plant.

8. False aralia (*Dizygotheca kerchoveana*)

S, Sh, 6'-8'

Often mistaken for marijuana. The deeply cut finger leaves are purplish. Feathery appearance with leaves most of the way to the bottom. Fertile, well-drained soils.

9. Frangipani (*Plumeria* spp.) CS, S-Sh, 6'-12'

Thick, wrist-size stems branch to unique shape and display the traditional Hawaiian lei flower in waxy red (*P. rubra*), white (*P. alba*), and yellowish (*P. obtusa*). Fragrant in summer months. Lance leaves fall in cool months. Protect from cold nights. Moderately salt-tolerant.

10. Heliconia (*Heliconia* spp.) S, S-Sh, 4'-8'

Sometimes called lobster claw or wild plantain and popular in Sarasota and other fairly frostless areas, this clump-grown perennial with miniature bananalike leaves produces colorful stalks which may be cut for indoor display. Many varieties are available.

11. Italian cypress (*Cupressus sempervirens*)

NC, S, 10'-20'

Narrow, columnar evergreen with formal appearance often seen in pairs or a staggered trio. Keep pruned short or will reach fifty feet and lower trunk will become bare. Spray for mites and fungus.

12. Jatropha coral plant (*Jatropha multifida*)

S, S-Sh, 6'-12'

Single trunk is topped in a feathery head of deeply cut leaves and brilliant coral red flower clusters. All jatrophas are poisonous if ingested.

13. Juniper (*Juniperus* spp.) NC, S, 6'-12'

Several species can be used as accent plants but you must choose a tall variety like Torulosa juniper or the Columnaris juniper. Evergreen needles need protection from mites and fungus.

14. Ligustrum (*L. lucidum*) NCS, S-Sh, 6'-12'

This common hedge plant is easily shaped as a single-trunk specimen tree. Thin out so inner limbs will show or prune into huge, bonsai-appearing pompoms. Keep topped or it will grow to 35 feet. Dislikes wet feet.

15. Loquat (*Eriobotrya japonica*) NCS, S, 10'-15'

Handsome, single-trunk tree with well-formed head, large grayish leaves, white flower clusters in fall, and delicious yellow fruit in late winter. Fruit the size of a golf ball. This hardy choice is one of the best small trees we have.

16. Norfolk Island pine (*Araucaria excelsa*)*

CS, S, 10'-40'

Unique spoked evergreen limbs from single trunk make this popular as a tub plant. For accents they need space to attain large height. Spray for fungus and mites periodically.

17. Pampas grass (*Cortaderia selloana*)*

NCS, S-Sh, 6'-8'

A perennial grass growing in huge clumps. Produces tall stalks of feathery silver plumes in summer. Plumes are cut for indoor decorations. Females are most showy.

18. Papyrus (*Cyperus* spp.) NCS, S-Sh, 2'-8'

Many species of galingale available with long, straight stems in clumps bearing a cluster of lanceolate leaves at the top. Plant in the edge of a water garden for tropical, aquatic effect or in accent tubs of moist soil. Papyrus is C. *papyrus*, a tall plant with wirelike leaves. The medium-height umbrella plant (C. *alternifolius*) has flat leaves. For miniature water garden use C. *haspan* 'Viviparus,' or C. *diffusus*.

19. Poinsettia (*Euphorbia pulcherrima*)

NCS, S, 6'-10'

The popular Christmas plant grows easily outdoors but is killed to the ground by frost. Plant behind permanent shrubs; prune in April, June, and August for full showing in winter. Don't let lights from a porch or window shine on poinsettia at night. Available with huge, colorful bracts in red, white, pink, and in doubles.

20. Ponytail (*Beaucarnea recurvata*) CS, S, 6'-12'

Miniature palm effect but with curious, huge, swollen trunk base that resembles a basketball half planted. Use as conversation piece in tub where trunk base can be seen or in a rock garden. If the head is severed while young, it will produce a multiheaded version.

21. Schefflera (*Brassaia actinophylla*)

CS, S-Sh, 10'-20'

Huge, shiny, umbrellalike leaves along single or many trunks. Prune for best show. Popular house plant, tub plant, or for accent. Protect from cold. In south Florida, larger plants produce spokes of small red flowers clustered above the foliage.

22. Screw pine (*Pandanus utilis*)* S, S-Sh, 10'-20'

Attractive, branching limbs bear tufts of long, pointed leaves whose margins are serrated and reddish. Produces fruits and large flowers that hang from stout stems. It boasts a unique root system that begins to branch out above ground level to give screw pine the appearance of walking. A curious plant indeed. Variegated forms are *P. veitchii* and *P. sanderi*.

23. Spanish bayonet (*Yucca aloifolia*)

NCS, S-Sh, 10'-20'

Dangerously sharp, lance leaves grow up and down a thick, herbaceous trunk. Landscape uses: good barrier to keep out pests or people, desert appearance for cactus garden or rock garden, highly salt-tolerant for sandy beach plantings. Gorgeous panicles of white, waxy flowers plunge from the top in springtime.

CACTI AND SUCCULENTS

Though not an arid state like Arizona and New Mexico whose southern borders grow the world's greatest collection of cacti, Florida does grow a sufficient number of dry climate plants for those who prefer the desert or rock garden landscape. Most require well-drained soil, medium fertility, and full sun to produce showy flowers.

Larger cacti are becoming more common in the marketplace due to chain stores shipping them in from the Southwest. These cacti are all related to two principal genera, *Opuntia* and *Cereus*.

The following outline will help you identify cacti and succulents in the Florida landscape.

I. OPUNTIA—Warts have a fine fuzz on top. The arms are jointed.

  A. Prickly pear*—Jointed segments are flat and resemble Mickey Mouse ears. The fruit are edible. Many species exist.

  B. Cholla—Pronounced "cho-yuh." The segments are like sausage links or cylinders. The fruit are not edible. Several species are common:

    1. Teddy bear—A "jumping cholla" with a mass of thistle-white needles that appear soft but are loosely attached and easily stick in your hand.

    2. Chain fruit—Another "jumping cholla" that grows new fruit at the end of last year's fruit, making a chain. Grows to ten feet with an equal spread.

    3. Staghorns—Thin branches are less spiny and resemble the antlers of a deer.

II. CEREUS*—Pronounced "serious." The arms are not jointed and they bloom at night. The warts that house the stickers are bald.

  A. Saquaro—Slow-growing giant. Arizona's state flower. Usually single trunk in Florida, with shallow vertical grooves. This lord of the desert lives 50 years. Stickers are straight and stiff.

Hardy prickly pear, an Opuntia cactus with edible fruit and sharp prickles.

  B. Old man—Numerous low-attached arms with deep vertical grooves that make starlike cross sections. Common in Florida. Large attractive flowers borne along the sides of the arms early in the morning. Tops of older branches have matted white bristles like gray hair.

  C. Night-blooming cereus—Inch-thick vine seen growing up tree trunks. Not attractive but has the most beautiful flowers in the cactus world, a saucer-sized, many petaled star with intense fragrance. Blooms only a few nights in summer. Root has an edible turnip.

Cereus cactus with its late-night bloom lingering into the early morning.

Twenty-foot Cereus cactus growing in central Florida.

Succulent aloe garden of Mr. and Mrs. Harold C. Anderson, St. Petersburg, displays many varieties.

Succulents *Pilea* (l), *Kalanchoe* (r), *Aloe* (rear) make low-maintenance dish gardens.

III. MISCELLANEOUS CACTI—The following are closely related to cereus cacti.
  A. Barrel cactus—Stickers are flat and hooked instead of straight. Cactus looks wrapped in a heavy mesh. Center holds pithy mass of thirst-quenching fluid. Flowers borne in a ring at the top.
  B. Pincushion—Resembles an egg covered with fine wooly bristles, light-colored with dark, hooked needles protruding from the wooly coat. This cactus is small but its flowers are large.
  C. Pineapple—This species has a criss-cross pattern that makes it resemble a pineapple.

IV. SUCCULENTS—Hundreds of miscellaneous, noncactus plants grow in the desert, store water in their succulent stems, and are often armed with sharp leaves or other protective structures.
  A. Yucca—One of the largest genera. Mother of the desert whose many pointed succulent leaves provide fiber for twine and Indian baskets, protection and food for rodents and cattle, as well as organic material and fertilizer for desert colonies. In Florida yucca is common with bayonet-protected trunks to ten feet or more. The beautiful, waxy flower in clusters borne atop spikes is the state flower of New Mexico. Like all cacti and succulents, they do not like wet feet.
  B. Century plant—Similar to yucca but the larger rosette of broad pointed leaves grows on the ground with no trunk. Gray-green and yellow variegated species are common in Florida, both with thorns along the leaves. Botanically it is named *Agave*. Used to make tequila and other potent drinks. Flowers appear on top of telephone pole stalks about five to ten years after young divisions are set out. Aboveground plant parts die after flowering. Cut stalks when young if you want to save your agave.

C. Aloe*—Attractive rosettes in many variegated species. The plump, lance-shaped leaves often have soft spines and are filled with a medicinal sap. Many grow to clumps two or three feet tall and bear showy spikes of flowers in shades of red and yellow.

D. Euphorbia—Several common species with milk sap. Crown of thorns (E. *milii*) has two-foot clumps of prickly spikes and showy little flowers. Pencil tree (E. *tirucalli*)* looks like a leafless tree with green, pencil-sized branching stems. Grows to fifteen feet. Milkstripe plant (E. *lactea*) resembles a night-blooming cereus to ten or twelve feet. Has three- or four-angled stems with brown stickers and yellow stripes at the center.

E. Stapelia—Also called carrion flower. A cactus-looking ground cover with four-angled, soft stems that branch and curve upward to about eight inches. Brownish, star-shaped flowers smell like dead fish.

F. Devil's backbone—*Pedilanthus tithymaloides* has green zig-zag stems holding marbled leaves and red, slipper-looking flowers. Grows to about five feet.

G. Dish garden plants*—A number of smaller succulents are available for dish gardens or miniature cactus gardens. Look for *Hawarthia*, *Echeveria*, *Sedum*, *Sanseveria*, *Aloe*, *Cryptanthus*, *Pilea*, *Crassula*, and *Kalanchoe*.

V. OTHERS—An assortment of additional plants look good in rock gardens where cacti and succulents are grown. See under accent plants: frangipani, bird of paradise, dracena, ponytail, papyrus, pampas grass, screw pine. And under ground covers: billbergia, oyster plant, peperomia, purple queen, society garlic, wandering Jew, liriope, mondo grass, and artillery plant.

Strawberry jar collection of *Sedum*, *Echeveria Kalanchoe*, *Aloe* (clockwise from lower left).

A mature pencil tree spreads its leafless limbs along this Key West street.

Dozens of delicious fruits hang from this mature tropical mango tree which doubles as a wind break.

PLANTS WITH EDIBLE FRUIT

NCS = planting zone
6'-10' = heights commonly seen
* = photo

A great diversity of shrubs and trees with deliciously edible fruit are available to the Florida landscaper. Both tropicals and Florida-adapted varieties of northern plants are available. In general, fruiting plants tend to be higher in maintenance. Choose a well-drained planting site to which organic matter and natural organic fertilizer such as manure have been added. Diagnose pests quickly and spray accordingly. Many fruits can be covered with a clear plastic bag sealed at the stem with a rubber band once the fruit is set to protect it from pests and predators. Fertilize all fruit-bearing plants with a low nitrogen fertilizer such as 4-6-8 in the spring, summer, and fall. Most fruiting plants produce better when grown in full sun.

1. Apple (*Malus* spp.)   NCS, 10'-15'
Deciduous tree, should be grafted. Good varieties for Florida include Anna, Dorsett Golden, Magnolia, Ein Shemer, San Piero, and Green Ischia.

2. Avocado (*Persea americana*)   CS, 20'-30'
These handsome shade trees (called "alligator pears" by early settlers) keep their leaves all year. Large fruit may be reddish, green, or black. Because of pollination problems best fruiting is achieved by planting a morning bloomer such as Taylor or Lulu (both hardy in central Florida) along with an afternoon bloomer like Hall (slightly less hardy). Any variety will produce fruit in south Florida. Spray in February and November for white fly and fungus.

3. Banana (*Musa* spp.)   CS, 10'-15'
Clumps with succulent stems and six-foot-long leaves split from wind make this a real tropical asset to any landscape. Divide clumps and plant in wet location. Protect from frost. Fruit are small.

4. Berries   NCS
Berries are available in great abundance in Florida. Some are small shrubs while others are vines. Popular plants include grapes, blackberries (thorny), blueberries (north Florida), strawberries, Chinese gooseberries, Barbados cherries (shrub called *malpighia*), and raspberries. Ask for Florida varieties and an info sheet of care of each berry you buy.

5. Carambola (*Averrhoa carambola*) CS, 15'-20'
Purchase only grafted ones. These produce delicious, yellow, oval fruits the size and texture of a pear and are called "star fruit" because of the shape of their cross section. I throw a handful of galvanized nails in planting holes to provide the zinc these small trees seem to like.

6. Coconut (*Cocos nucifera*)*   S, 30'-60'

These majestic palms of south Florida have sweeping trunks and a mass of football-shaped fruit that drops or can be picked green or ripe almost any time of year. Both the pulp and the milk in the inner seed are prized. Coconut palms look especially nice grown in clusters.

7. Fig (*Ficus carica*)   NCS, 6'-12'

Eat skin and all of this brown, golf-ball-sized soft fruit. The leaves are large and deciduous. Florida varieties include Celeste, Alma, San Piero and Brown Turkey. Prune as a shrub or small tree.

8. Guava (*Psidium* spp.)   CS, 10'-20'

The Cattley guava (*P. cattleianum*) has two-inch fruit. Red ones are sweeter than the acidic yellow fruits. The common guava (*P. guajava*), "Florida's peach," is yellow-skinned and grows up to six inches. Hand-eaten, juiced, jellied, canned, or made into pies or ice cream. A versatile fruit.

9. Loquat (*Eriobotrya japonica*)   NCS, 15'-20'

Well-shaped, small tree with evergreen leaves and clusters of yellow fruit, which are delicious eaten out of hand in late winter.

10. Lychee (*Litchi chinensis*)   CS, 20'-30'

Compact head of large, glossy leaves, quite attractive. Small round fruits are colorful red and have a sweet tropical taste and the texture of a grape. Peel the skin and eat in later summer.

11. Macadamia (*M. ternifolia*)   S, 20'-30'

Handsome, evergreen tree with long, dark leaves bears moderately in Florida. The crisp, sweet nut has a hard shell which is difficult to crack (use vise grips).

12. Mango (*Mangifera indica*)*   CS, 20'-40'

This tropical shade tree has fruit the size of a softball that is eaten fresh and popular in salads, custards, and ice cream. Your first bite of mango should be a small one. Some are allergic to its flesh. Likes rich soil.

13. Mulberry (*Moros* spp.)   NC, 20'-30'

Deciduous and hardy against cold, the blackberry-looking fruit could make a mess over sidewalks and drives. Grafted trees are better. The fruit is eaten out of hand or made into preserves or pies.

14. Papaya (*Carica papaya*)   CS, 15'-20'

Borne in clusters on female plants, the large fruit has meat a little like canteloupe but with a strong, tropical flavor. Plant a male or bisexual plant nearby to pollinate the female. Trees grow and bear in one year and die after five or six years, so keep planting.

15. Peach (*Amygdalus persica*)   NCS, 15'-20'

Great-tasting fruit but you should always plant Florida varieties like Flordasun, Flordagold, Flordawon, Flordabelle, McRed, or Early Amber. For fuzz-free fruit plant a Sunred nectarine. Leaves fall in winter and need protective sprays in summer.

16. Pear (*Pyrus serotina*)   NCS, 10'-15'

Plant Hood, Carnes, Baldwin, Kieffer, Pineapple, LeConte, or Orient. Slow grower, deciduous, and has an upright, ornamental shape.

17. Pecan (*Carya illinoensis*)   NC, 30'-40'

Fertilize often and spray for zinc deficiency to get maximum nuts. Protect against tent caterpillars and plant only Florida varieties such as Curtis, Moneymaker, and Desirable. Deciduous.

18. Persimmon (*Diospyros kaki*)   NC, 10'-12'

Leaves fall in winter. Plant Florida varieties including Hanafuyu, Fuyu, Hazakume, O'Gosho, Saijo, Tanenashi, Tamopan, and Hachiya.

19. Plum (*Prunus salicinas*)   NC, 10'-20'

Another deciduous tree that likes cross-pollination, especially from native wild plum. Plant Excelsior and Abundance in central Florida. Almost any variety does well in north Florida.

20. Pineapple (*Ananas comosus*)   CS, 1'-2'

A prickly ground cover with long spiny fingers. A pinch of calcium carbide in the center will cause it to grow a pineapple. Then the old plant dies. Dislikes salt air, limestone soils, excess water, and drafts.

21. Pomegranate (*Punica granatum*)   NC, 10'-15'

Fruit the size of a softball contains hundreds of seeds covered with a sweet, red flesh. Tree or shrub is deciduous.

22. Sapodilla (*Achras zapota*)   S, 20'-30'

Symmetrical broadleaf evergreen with large attractive leaves bears brown fruit, 3-4 inches in diameter, in later summer. Very salt-tolerant.

23. Sapote (*Calocarpum sapota*)   S, 20'-40'

Older trees take a light freeze. Young ones don't. Oval fruits 4 or 5 inches long are a scaly brown and mature in early summer. Eat fresh or use in marmalades and sherbets. Other names appear for mamey sapote, black, green and white sapote. All are tropical.

24. Surinam cherry (*Eugenia uniflora*)   CS, 10'-20'

Large, bushy hedge shrub bearing evergreen leaves red when new. Bears red-orange cherries, ribbed vertically, that look like little pumpkins. Eat fresh for a bouncy, sweet taste.

In concluding this plant description reference chapter it is helpful to note that many plants are used or avoided in the landscape because they have a unique quality: they attract birds, are poisonous, are highly salt-tolerant, and so on. Following are some lists that will serve as a reference to landscapers looking for plants that fit into these particular situations.

Dense, woodsy plantings with lots of undergrowth give birds the kind of protection they seek. Include seed bearers like palms and oaks.

PLANTS THAT ATTRACT BIRDS

For those home owners who like to attract and observe birds there are plants available whose seeds or fruit provide nourishment for the birds. Plant several of these species. Also, provide water in a bird bath, bird feeders when plants are not fruiting, and bird houses to provide nesting grounds. Remember each bird species prefers a special house. Refer to the Florida Audubon Society or your County Extension office for helpful brochures. Birds like lots of shrubs and trees in a yard free of cats. Here is a partial list of bird-attracting plants to incorporate in your landscape.

TREES:

cabbage palm (*Sabal palmetto*), camphor (*Cinnamomum camphora*), Canary Island date palm (*Phoenix canariensis*), cherry laurel (*Prunus caroliniana*), chinaberry (*Melia ozedarach*), citrus, dogwood (*Cornus florida*), holly (*Ilex opaca, I. cassine*), loquat (*Eriobotrya japonica*), magnolia (M. *grandiflora*), oaks (*Quercus spp.*)

SHRUBS:

beautyberry (*Callicarpa americana*), carissa (*C. grandiflora*), downy myrtle (*Rhodomyrtus tomentosa*), elderberry (*Sambucus simpsonii*), feijoa (*F. sellowiana*), firethorn (*Pyracantha coccinea*), golden dewdrop (*Duranta repens*), grapes (*Vitus spp.*), hawthorn (*Crataegus floridana*), seagrape (*Coceoloba uvifera*), silverthorn (*Eleagnus pungens*), Surinam cherry (*Eugenia uniflora*), viburnum (*V. odoratissimum*), wax myrtle (*Myrica cerifera*), podocarpus (*Podocarpus spp.*)

PLANTS THAT ATTRACT BUTTERFLIES AND HUMMINGBIRDS

Butterfly bush (*Buddleia* spp.)
Cape honeysuckle (*Tecomaria capensis*)
Coral honeysuckle (*Lonicera sempervirens*)
Dwarf poinciana (*P. pulcherrima*)
Glorybower (*Clerodendron speciosissiumum*)
Hibiscus (H. *rosa-sinensis*)
Morning glory (*Ipomoea* spp.)
Pandora (*P. lanceolata*)
Plumbago (*P. capensis*)
Shrimp plant (*Beloperone guttata*).

SALT-TOLERANT PLANTS

Subdivided into categories, this list includes plants proven to be highly salt-tolerant, ones that withstand dune conditions. Many other plants not listed exhibit mild tolerance and can be planted a couple of blocks from salty shores. Check index for additional information on plants listed here.

TREES: Australian pine, black olive, buttonwood, carrotwood, cedar, geiger tree, Jerusalem thorn, Norfolk Island pine, pigeon plum, pine, pitch apple, punk, sea hibiscus, wax myrtle.

SHRUBS: acacia, bottlebrush, carissa, century plant, cocoplum, dracena, *Elaeagnus*, lantana, ligustrum, oleander, pencil tree, pittosporum, pyracantha, salt bush, sea grape, yaupon holly.

PALMS: cabbage palm, coconut, Washington palm.

GROUND COVERS: caltrope, *Euonymous fortunai*, fig marigold, ivy, lantana (weeping), sanseveria, sedum, shore juniper, Virginia creeper, wedelia, winter creeper.

VINES: creeping fig, flame vine, goat's foot morning glory, night-blooming cereus, trumpet vine, winter creeper.

POISONOUS PLANTS IN THE LANDSCAPE

In Florida, many common and beautiful landscape plants, like poinsettia and allamanda, are poisonous. And some, like ochrosia, have delicious-looking fruit. Here's an easy rule: "Don't eat it unless you are sure." That goes for mushrooms too. If you like mushrooms, buy them at the grocery store. Here's another: "Be cautious of the sap in all plants." Don't chew on any stem or leaf. Some, like the common dieffenbachia seen in malls, potted in homes, and even doctor's offices, are lethal if you take a bite. Here is a partial list of some of Florida's poisonous landscape plants along with that part of the plant found to be toxic.

COMMON NAME	BOTANICAL	TOXIC PART
Allamanda, yellow	A. *cathartica*	fruit
Angel's trumpet	*Datura arborea*	all parts
Brazilian pepper (Florida holly)	*Schinus*	berries
Cherry laurel	*Prunus caroliniana*	leaves
Crape jasmine	*Ervatamia coronaria*	roots, bark, flowers
Crown of thorns	*Euphorbia milii*	sap
Dieffenbachia (Dumb cane)	*Dieffenbachia* spp.	sap
Gloriosa lily	*Gloriosa* spp.	all parts
Hydrangea	H. *macrophylla*	sap
Mango	*Mangifera indica*	fruit skin (sensitive people)
Oleander	*Nerium oleander*	all parts
Ochrosia	O. *elliptica*	fruit
Pencil cactus	*Euphorbia tirucalli*	sap
Poinsettia	*Euphorbia pulcherrima*	sap

NATIVE PLANTS OF FLORIDA

In this age of environmental awareness, pesticide misuse, and irrigation restrictions, many landscapers are selecting more and more native plants for their designs. Native plants grow and survive in the wilds of Florida. They are more tolerant of temperature changes, insect and disease pests, drought, excess rains, and poor soils than the many cultivated hybrids introduced to Florida. The following list contains several native plants useful for Florida landscapes. Many of these plants are protected by Florida laws from being dug out of the woods, so ask for them at licensed nurseries where they have been legally propagated.

TREES: red maple, bontia, black olive, gumbo limbo, redbud, satin leaf, pitch apple, sea grape, silver buttonwood, geiger tree, dogwood, mahoe sea hibiscus, American holly, red cedar, sweet gum, wild tamarind, Southern magnolia, slash pine, cherry laurel, live oak, mahogany, bald cypress.

SHRUBS: cocoplum, firebush, wax myrtle, inkberry, yaupon holly, pitch apple, seven-year apple, varnish-leaf, Spanish stopper, wild coffee, Florida flame azalea, Southern swamp azalea, sea lavender, Spanish bayonet.

PALMS: paurotis palm, silver palm, Sargent cherry palm, royal palm, cabbage palm, saw palmetto, brittle thatch palm, Jamaica thatch palm.

GROUND COVERS: gopher apple, beach morning-glory, dwarf lantana, partridge berry, peperomia, puncture vine, coontie, wandering Jew, bromeliads, maidenhair fern, Boston fern, goldfoot fern, giant brake, spider lily, zephyr lilies.

VINES: trumpet creeper, swamp lily, Carolina yellow jessamine, Virginia creeper.

Oleander, the most common and most poisonous shrub in the Florida landscape.

Index

Boldface page numbers refer to plant descriptions.